MAKE ROOM FOR GOD

MAKE ROOM FOR GOD

The Spirituality of Awakening

Dear Suzanne,
Blessings and love,
Sr. Germaine

M. Germaine Hustedde, PHJC

Copyright © 2012 by M. Germaine Hustedde, PHJC.

Library of Congress Control Number:		2012920876
ISBN:	Hardcover	978-1-4797-5687-2
	Softcover	978-1-4797-4609-5
	Ebook	978-1-4797-4610-1

This book was printed in the United States of America.

To order additional copies of this book, contact:
Xlibris Corporation
1-888-795-4274
www.Xlibris.com
Orders@Xlibris.com
125471

CONTENTS

DEDICATION

For all the Boys who have been or will be
Members of the Family of St. Joseph Home-
"Caring Place"
Mitunguu (Meru) Kenya
And for all who continue this ministry
With love.

FOREWARD

ON OCCASION, AS we were growing up, we took a longer journey to Belleville or St. Louis to visit family or relatives. It was not unusual shortly after we were on the way, to hear one or other of the siblings query, "Dad, are we there yet?" The journey was not that long, but it seemed interminable to small children. Mother always found a way to distract us and make the long drive seem to go faster.

In the journey through life, we can experience something of the same impatience to reach the goal for which we strive. However, life's companions and the great God whom we seek, have ways of nurturing and accompanying us along the way. We need but be awake to the nuances of light and dark that give depth and meaning as the times passes.

In the allegorical work of Richard Bach, Jonathan Livingston Seagull, more than anything else, wants to excel in flying. He wants to fly further and faster, more gracefully and higher than any of his feathered colleagues had ever done. Eventually Jonathan discovers that there are boundaries he cannot surpass, limits to the speed he can attain and the heights he can ascend. The moral which concludes the second part of the allegory is that the only limits we face are those we place upon ourselves.

Our daily experience indicates that this is not entirely the case. I discover in myself, through my everydayness, that my freedom is limited by my embodiment, my characteristic emotionality as well as by my temperamental bent, etc.,—limited, yes! But not totally and irrevocably defined!

In the realm of the spiritual I can far exceed the confines of time and space. I am free to scale the heights, to probe the depths and to relish the discoveries that I find in the foreign territory of myself. It is in this unexplored realm that I make room for God and uncover the tasty morsels of spiritual awakening.

While my senses keep my world alive, I know too, that someday these very attributes will fall to the limits of death. Only the spiritual dimension of self will prevail and that which was shrouded in mystery will be revealed. In that truth I will live for all eternity.

This book attempts to underscore the awareness and conviction that God is the "Still Point" of my life and that awakening to this marvelous truth in striving for holiness and wholeness will pay dividends beyond my greatest expectations. God is the ultimate Source of my being. Christ is our Brother and Friend and it is through the outpouring of the Holy Spirit $^{(Acts\ 2:33)}$ that we are led ever more deeply into the core of self where we experience the abiding Presence of the Trinity and the power of the Resurrection to help us reach our goal.

Pentecost shapes us for a constant attitude of being "toward" God so that we recognize always that God is the Ground of our Being. The life we are given through the power of the Holy Spirit is foundational to our dignity and our becoming.

The contents of this work have been carried with me in mind and heart through many years. In four continents I have experienced both beauty and appreciation for the gift of life as well as the truth that every human person seeks for the True and the Beautiful . . . for the Something greater than self. In other instances I have seen the disregard and degradation forced upon the helpless and marginalized of our world. It is in awakening to God's gifts and blessings that we come to know that living is precious and that harshness and dissonance can meld into a harmonic whole and grace me, and those around me, with peace and joy in living when God is welcomed into the picture.

This book is fashioned on the idea and ideal of Formative Spirituality. We do not reach our goal all at once, but pursue the journey through every stage of life. Each stage is a building block enabling me to climb further into the pursuit of growing into God and welcoming the Triune Godhead into my life. Formation in the truest sense means to bring to light and life, the gifts which God in his gracious goodness has so generously conferred upon us.

ACKNOWLEDGMENTS

GOD, CONSTANT COMPANION and Giver of life receives my first and deepest thanks!

It is my grateful duty to thank my parents who taught me from childhood that there are values in this world that cannot be bought. They instilled in me the awareness that God is the Provider and Sustainer of the Gift of my life and that our family circle was big enough to always welcome God. I thank my brothers and sisters who were my first source of knowing, experientially, the joy of living.

I am grateful to my Congregation, the Poor Handmaids of Jesus Christ, and to Sister Nora Hahn, Provincial, for encouragement and for allowing me the time to pursue this topic. I owe an immeasurable debt of gratitude to my mentor and friend, Dr. Susan Annette Muto of the Epiphany Foundation for taking the time to critique the entire draft and proffer valuable suggestions for its improvement. I thank Katie Amick of our Communication Department for her assistance in formatting the text and Sisters Marlene Ann Lama and Virginia Kampwerth for advice and encouragement. I gratefully acknowledge the wonderful support I have received from Mr. & Mrs. Benedict Koch that has helped to make this venture a reality.

I would certainly be amiss, if I did not thank the Sisters of the various Provinces of the Congregation of the Poor Handmaids of Jesus Christ where I have been able to minister. Their valuable example of living with joy and gratitude and relishing the Gift of Life that God has so generously afforded each of us has enriched my journey. These include our American Province, the Sisters of the Generalate and Province—Germany, the Indian Province and Region Kenya.

The graphics used throughout are the work of Sister Roswindis Sauerwald, PHJC of our German Province. They are used with permission and my gratitude.

I am grateful for all the formative experiences I have had because of God's loving Providence. Some stand out more boldly than others. Among these I include years of study in the Institute of Formative Spirituality, Duquesne University, the opportunity to have ministered in cultures other than my own, through which I have met and made steadfast friends in many countries of God's beautiful planet. Each has given me a wealth that defies words.

The experience that welds the reality of "Making Room for God—the Spirituality of Awakening" in the depth of my being is the profound change I have experienced in Kenya in working with the boys who were homeless and living on the Streets. Their resiliency and transformation, sincerity and example would warm every heart. It is primarily for their future that I pray for the success of this book.

Donaldson, Indiana—July, 2012
M. Germaine Hustedde, PHJC

CHAPTER ONE

IN EARTHEN VESSELS

I HAVE ALWAYS BEEN fascinated by the potter's wheel. Perhaps it is the completed object that attracts me, though there is a fascination for me in the art itself.

The lump of clay upon the wheel is just a lump—wet, sticky, shapeless. The first soft whirring hum of motion initiates the lifeless, inert mass into the process of becoming. Slowly the deft fingers of the craftsman shape and form the clay. Now and again a bit of momentum is given to the "dying" wheel. The rotating movement and centering are of paramount importance if the object is to turn out just right. There must be no hesitation or delay now that the work is begun. If the clay were to dry and harden it would be impossible to form. Now it is supple, malleable, soft and receptive. It is thrilling to see an object or vessel emerge. Through the nimble dexterity of the potter, the clay is shaped and molded into a creation which the potter has in mind. The clay just doesn't happen to become *this* "pot". However, potentially it *is* this piece of pottery when the potter places this lump of clay upon the wheel.

The Self—Becoming

My emerging self is somewhat analogous to the potter and the clay. It is also resonant of the message given to Prophet Jeremiah whom the Lord bade to betake himself to the potter's house. Jeremiah obeyed the Lord's promptings and spoke to the people of Israel in parable. "Like clay in the hands of the potter, so are you in my hand . . ."[1]

It seems very appropriate to consider the event of Pentecost in connection with ourselves as vessels of clay. Continuing the analogy, those gathered in that Upper room that first Pentecost (Acts 2:1-20) experienced the process of being "fired" in the kiln Divine Love. The Spirit descended upon all who were gathered and confirmed them in strength, durability and unbreakable faith. Until the 'firing' process is complete the 'green ware' is very susceptible to breakage, chipping and flaws of every sort. The event of Pentecost sent a 'fire' upon those gathered and the earth that has never been, nor can be extinguished. We are the earth of which the Lord said, "I have come to cast fire upon the earth and what better wish can I have than that it should be kindled." (Lk. 12:49)

It is in this reality that each of us finds the strength, wisdom and delight in making room for God in our lives. It is the Spirit who gives life in all its fullness. From birth until death, the self as a dynamic whole, is always emerging, and always in the hands of the Divine Potter. God's gift to me is the fact that I have life and that life is always striving *to become.* This experience of self in the process of emerging, unfolds in the variety of experiences which make up my daily life. Day by day the potential '**me**' unfolds.

Our "unfolding" is within a given time and place. Gabriel Marcel says that "the essence of [person] is to be in a situation".[2] Indeed, we are always in a concrete, specific, situation in our world. The milieu into which I was born, my homeland, religious and political convictions, work, talent, emotions—all of life's situations contribute to my unfolding and hold me in a framework of "situatedness". The circumstances I find myself in, along with my attitude toward them, gives meaning in a positive or negative stance to the situatedness of my life. But life always unfolds against the backdrop of the Holy—whether I am conscious of it or not! It is precisely in these situations that I find God or I do not find Him at all!

As Marcel ponders his notion of our 'being in a situation', he incorporates the ideas of **empty** and **full.** He thus comes to describe **"being"** as fullness.[3] We spend our days waiting for our dreams, hopes and desires to be fulfilled. When nothing matters or has importance for us, our attention is disparate, and interest is lacking. We become lethargic and listless. The world seems to answer us in a mechanical way and life is running on the gauge of **empty.** We have lost the prime focus of our lives.

Years ago, as I was out west for a short space of time with a friend, I read a small, but tragic, account in a newspaper. The details have long escaped me but the essence of the account remains strikingly in my mind. One evening, a very wealthy young woman checked into a hotel and was found dead the next morning. She had 'checked out' of life. She left a short suicide note that read in part, and remains vividly with me: "I'm tired of going through life clapping with one hand". Such was her emptiness that she chose not to continue embracing the life that God had given her. Unless we are creative, life-giving people we can easily come to the conclusion that life is not worth living. It is true! We cannot make an impression in life "clapping with one hand"! Are we only beating the air? What is there of essence, about the way we live? Marcel says, "Such experiences are the very negation of feelings of fullness and profusion that we feel on other occasions." Unless I try to incorporate a stance of acceptance toward the situations that come into my life, and see them all as coming from the hand of Providence, I may grow resentful, and allow time and circumstances to disfigure me. Movements toward silence and thoughtful reflection may be the ingredients necessary for a positive attitude, the ingredients for keeping my life in perspective. These help establish stability and meaningfulness in our emerging. We must search for the "why" of our lives. Frankl, quoting Nietzsche, in "***Man's Search for Meaning***" states aptly, "He who has a *why* to live for can bear almost any how." Frankl's victory over the sadistic conditions in the Nazi concentration camp bears this out.[4]

Make a Gift of Life

A simple prayer card, created by the Abbey Press says very aptly, "We cannot make a success of our life without making a gift of it." Perhaps, I am not in a position to make large donations, impressive speeches or magnificent inventions. None such is what it means to make a **gift of my life.** There are myriad other chances that avail me. Perhaps I am a good listener. Some elderly person may need a companion now and then. Maybe I have the ability to comfort someone who experiences the loss of a loved one. Can I reach out to a frightened child or an anxious adult who faces an unexpected hospital ordeal?

Gifting my life means that I never lose sight of the mission I have to use my abilities, be they ever so small, to reach out in love, care and affection to those around me and beyond my immediate horizon. Situations around me and in the broader context, will not call me forth, unless, with God's grace I am ever willing to gift another out of the resources of my life.

There are many examples in real life of how this giftedness is played out. Consider a man with the talent of George Washington Carver. We know that he was born a slave and struggled against distressing odds to get a good education. Through perseverance and trust in God, despite even abuse and prejudice along the way, Carver finally graduated with a Master's Degree and subsequently was offered a coveted teaching position in the University of Iowa. Though he was loved and appreciated at the university, eventually Carver joined the great humanitarian, Booker T. Washington, to assist him in educating the black folk in the south. Carver found meaning there among the poor in the parched cotton fields. Though later, he was offered a fine office and a lucrative salary for his discoveries, he turned down the offers. Many folks were mystified by his rejection of such great monetary advancement. Critics cajoled him saying, "If you had all that money, you could help so many of your people." Caver's response was, "If I had a lot of money, I might forget."

Isn't it true that we often live in forgetfulness? We forget the Giver. We forget that the Spirit is the Force for Good in our lives. Carver always attributed his intelligence, his success and ability to the Lord. If I depend only on my own wisdom, assets and abilities, I am really playing out the scenario of "one hand clapping." Remembering God and His Divine intervention in everything, changes all effort into a partnership. God will not be outdone in generosity. Carver knew and understood implicitly that life only makes sense when it is inner directed to the Holy and outer directed to the other.

Situations in life have a kind of hidden, intrinsic power to squeeze the meaning out of life or to bolster its worth, beauty and determination . . ."to make a gift of it". Of themselves, situations have no power at all over me. I am the meaning-giver! By allowing myself to be completely wrapped up in the situations of the moment on the physical level, I negate authentic engagement or commitment. Van Ewijk compares such a life to a set of beads "which neatly laid out one next to the other give the impression of forming a necklace, but on being touched roll away in all directions; they do not form a connective whole because I have overlooked the thread—the meaning of life."[5]

Intrinsic Value

My genuine worth consists in my being. Every individual who has ever lived, or will live, is a unique creation of the God of Life . . . precious, loved and valuable by reason of existence. The things I can do or accomplish, mental acumen or lack of it, do not add or detract from the value I am in myself. What another may think of me is not really all that important, for another person can neither diminish nor increase my true worth, or genuine value. Our Lord tells us quite plainly through the Prophet Isaiah, "You are precious in my eyes and I love you."[6] It is not in the doing that one finds joy, but in the joy with which I perform the task at hand, recognizing that every gift I possess is an expression and extension of God's love for me. Herein is our intrinsic worth!

Every human person is a "being" constituted by his/her situation within the world. We are primarily situated in our humanness—the body, which at the same time is in a spatial relationship to our world. It is through the body, with its senses and abilities, that I come to personal realization. We cannot think of disembodied attitudes! My life, however, is not identical with my body. In prayerful recollection, a thoughtful ingathering, one rises above any dichotomy, separation or polarity that may haunt us. In looking lovingly, with an inward gaze, one concludes that "I am more than my physical life". I gain a sense of my existence by recognizing the divine Source of my being.

The pottery paradigm is applicable here, too. Consider again the formless lump of clay thrust upon the potter's wheel. It is our human tendency to admire the shape and form of the vessel which emerges, from its outward dimensions. However, the potter shapes and fashions the clay conscious of the space within. We look at the confines of the vase, the orifice of the piece of pottery, but the space within is equally important. The receptivity of the vase or vessel is defined by its outer limits. All my appreciation of the shape, size, color and design of the pottery cannot change the genuine space within nor alter the pottery in any way. Its identity is fixed as this specific piece of pottery and no other.

Humanness subjects me to the limitations of time and space—outer dimensions, but I am not imprisoned there! I can rise above and beyond these temporal confinements to the deeper aspects of life. If the human person is likened to the vessel of clay, we can be sure that that same vessel is transformed in Baptism through the indwelling of the Holy Spirit. We are filled with new life, a new wine, as it were—just as at the Wedding of Cana. In a sense, with this new life I can take wings and fly! Marcel regards fidelity, hope and love as elements which help the human person to realize one's self. Basically, these are the same graces we find in the perusal of Scripture, necessary to come to the fullness of life. The underlying concept of the biblical view of life is the creation of humankind in God's image. This divine likeness becomes our vehicle for attaining that fullness of life which Jesus promised, "I have come that you may have **life** and have it to the full".[7] And the great Father of the Church, Iranaeus exclaimed, "the glory of God is [humankind] fully alive." He added to that thought that we are the work of God and it is God who shapes us. We should therefore be tractable clay in the hands of the Divine Potter and keep the form that God designs for us. To try to become something or someone that God does not have in His plan for me would be disastrous.

Fullness of Life

Life in the biblical sense also means to live according to God's way. Leviticus 19:2 admonishes us "Be holy, for I the Lord, your God, am holy." Though we seldom acknowledge or attend to it, the pursuit of holiness is built into every human being God has ever created. We thirst for the good, the holy, the beautiful, as St. Augustine reminded us, and we are restless until we rest in God.

The fourteenth century anchoress and mystic, Julian of Norwich underscores this very reality in the fifth of her SHOWINGS: She says,

"It is necessary for us to know the littleness of creatures in order to reduce them to nothingness in our judgment, so that we may love and have the uncreated God. The reason we are not fully at ease in heart and soul is because we seek rest in these things that are so little and have no rest within them, and pay no attention to our God who is Almighty, All-wise, All-good, and the only rest."[8]

We are a journeying people in whom the ancient Exodus is daily repeated. When God brought His people from exile He empowered Moses to sate their human thirst from the rock and God supplied the life-sustaining manna as food for the weary travelers. We move from one plane of life, from one activity to another, from one indulgence to another, always seeking fulfillment, liberty, and satiety. In our search, we fail to recognize that these pursuits can never really satisfy. We experience our own alienation, exile and pitiful condition. It is the tendency of every human being to strain toward the Infinite! Our hunger and thirst for happiness and fulfillment is our radical tendency toward the all-loving God. Authentic hunger and thirst at the deepest center of myself, becomes an ardent desire to live in creative fidelity to, and with, our loving, living God, very basically—to make room for God in my life. van Croonenberg points out that "the dynamic flow of human life . . . subject to an ever changing situation and communion with the Absolute Thou is no exception." He goes on to instruct us that "it is only at the price of continuous struggle and utmost fidelity that one can break through the clouds of insecurity and arrive at the culminating point where we experience the presence of True Love."[9]

In our daily striving, we may attain a momentary sense of fulfillment. Likewise, a moment's reflection shows us how fleeting that fulfillment is. It is an up and down, now and then, vacillating movement. We never quite achieve the ability to remain at the peak. We hunger and thirst in the natural order because we long to continue our life. If the desire for God becomes strong enough we long to "die" because we know that in our limited earthly existence we cannot live fully. Fromm, the psychologist, contends that we come to die before we are fully born! Therefore, it behooves us to meet the daily 'deaths' which come into our lives magnanimously. Difficulties and setbacks which we experience every day help us to relinquish our tendencies to egoistic self-reliance and a sense of false pride, sufficiency and security. We hunger more and more for God who is all holy and just and our only authentic fulfillment.

Those who hunger and thirst after holiness and justice, grow in communion, oneness, and solidarity. We are nudged into a depth of meaning and wholeness which the pursuit of fame, riches and pleasure cannot provide. Christ becomes the food and drink that can satisfy us throughout out life's journey. As Durwell so rightly, asserts, we are ever on the march, not so much with feet, but with heart, longing and will.[10]

This Almighty and all-wise God is the God of the Covenant. Even today, God's covenant with us is His promise to sustain us. We are urged to actively seek a relationship with God. We need to look to the Lord as our strength and companion on every step of our journey. We cannot go the way alone! Only in Him will we find true peace and rest. He is the oasis in our human deserts.

Jesus is the mediator of the new Covenant. He ratified this through His death on Calvary. For God's covenant to be fully accomplished and effective, we must partner with Him. It beckons us to remember the wonderful things God has done for us and to live in wakeful, grateful fidelity

Notes:

1. Jeremiah 18:6 *

2. H.J. Blackman, Six Existentialist Thinkers, (New York: Harper & Row Publishers, 1959) p. 68.

3. Gabriel, Marcel, Metaphysical Journal, trans. by Bernard Wall (Chicago: Henry Regnery Company, 1952) p.206.

4. Viktor Frankl, Man's Search For Meaning—Revised and Updated, (New York: Washington Square Press, 1984) p.126

5. Thomas J.M. Van Ewijh, Gabriel Marcel—An Introduction (Glen Rock, New Jersey: Paulist Press, 1965), p.38.

6. Cf. Isaiah 43: 1-50. 7. John 10:10 8. M.L.del Mastro (trans.) The Revelation of Divine Love in Sixteen Showings—Made to Dame Julian of Norwich (Liguori, MO., Triumph Books, 1994), p.67.

9. Engelbert van Coonenburg, Gateway to Reality: An Introduction to Philosophy (Pittsburg, Duquesne University Press 1968) p.128.

10. Conf. F.X.Durwell, The Redeeming Christ: Toward a Theology of Spirituality, trans. By Rosemary Sheed (New York: Sheed and Ward, 1963), p.190.

*Scripture references, used throughout, are from the New American Bible, (Iowa Falls, Iowa: The World Bible Publishers, Inc.), 1991.

AWAKENING

THE SEARCH

Longing laps my soul
Like persistent tides.
Emptiness,
eager,
impatient to be filled—
clutches too quickly
the tempting morsels
that satisfy the restless self.
Alluring, gossamer clutter!

Heart smarts
And writhes in vain
To shed the pain
Of being gorged with
Nothingness.

I test the art
Of letting-go
That I may know
The persistent ache of my
Incompleteness.

And in my new found emptiness,
There is room for God!

FOR REFLECTION:

What are the tempting morsels that still allure me?

What is the experience like of being gorged with "nothingness"?

What will I change in my life to make room for God?

CHAPTER TWO

WITH HEART, LONGING AND WILL

A STORY IS told of a wise old rabbi. The gentleman was revered and respected by nearly all who knew him. Wisdom and powers of discernment had endeared him to most everyone with whom he came in contact.

For all his admirers, however, two young lads resented the goodness, wisdom and discretion of the old rabbi. Youthful blindness prompted the lads to attempt to disparage the reputation of the beloved man. They plotted to trick the rabbi so as to put him in a less favorable light. The plan was to present a newborn bird to the rabbi, but concealed within the palms of their cupped hands. They would test the wisdom and discernment of the rabbi by asking him to tell them if the bird was dead or alive. If the rabbi replied that the bird was alive, they would quickly deprive the frail, concealed creature of life. If the rabbi concluded that the bird was dead, they would reveal the featherless, frightened creature pulsing with life. Either way, the rabbi would appear in a bad light!

With their plans secure, the two lads approached the rabbi. "Is the bird, concealed in our hands, dead or alive?" came the triumphant query. A moment of deep thoughtfulness followed as the rabbi peered into the eyes of each of the boys. Then he smiled kindly and said, "The answer is in your hands!"

In a very true sense, the rabbi's answer applies to the life of each of us. The daily life situation in which we find ourselves can be life-giving or life-draining, dependent on the view I take, the mood I'm in, or the attitudes that govern most of my waking hours. Like the wise old rabbi concluded, "It is in our hands." I remember an incident that made a deep and lasting impression upon me. In a small village in Minnesota, one of the boys in the class suddenly became orphaned through a tragic accident in the family. Sister, felt great compassion for the lad and in the days that followed, she often spoke with the boy, sharing how concerned she was for him and how badly she felt for his loss. The boy, just barely a teenager surprised Sister by saying, "Sister, don't worry about me! God doesn't give us burdens that we cannot bear." What faith and what wisdom!!

The Drama of Life

All of life is a stage for the drama of living. Even from our present vantage point we can look back and ascertain the difference attitudes, circumstances and gratitude have played in our lives. When we approach life with a courageous heart and a deep longing to experience fulfillment we are more likely to reap those blessings. But so often we live in an attitude of forgetfulness. We take way too much for granted and expect too much in return. When I remember the blessings of my childhood and youth, I must "ooze" with gratitude. "Oh" perhaps you think, "Life must have been without cares or concern." Just the opposite! I was born in the Depression years and life generally was a struggle for everyone. Money was not enough, crops failed, sand and windstorms destroyed, what was, the hopes of a harvest. Visiting school and church were the "workouts" that now take place in gyms and spas. Our daily "footing" of approximately six miles wore out many a pair of shoes, though in the Spring, Summer and Fall we were admonished to spare them by walking barefoot.

Practically every day of my young life, I pestered my mother for permission to take piano lessons. The gentle, but firm reply was always the same: "Child, there is not enough money." It never once occurred to me that we also did not have an instrument at home on which I could practice!

The long summer holiday from school was a lesson in home-making and horticulture. Since there was no grocery store anywhere close around, bread making, canning and gardening were the order of the day. We siblings vied for the end slices of the fresh homemade bread but we also learned the art of baking, with practice and Mother's patience. Hours in the fresh air and sunshine weeding and harvesting grapes, rhubarb, and vegetables of every sort filled the morning hours. Some days, mornings were given to canning and preserving the rich harvest and vegetables. Afternoons were a time for recreation. With no TV, iPods or even a radio, because electricity had not yet come to our rural area, we entertained ourselves. Favorite spots were the huge old mulberry tree in the front yard and the clump of forest down in the pasture near the little "Branch". The mulberry tree had a fascination about it because the whole inner trunk had burnt away and one could actually scramble in and out of the tree trunk. The mini-forest was just on the edge of the small stream where alternately we could climb trees and swing in their branches or just wade to our hearts content in the cool waters. All too soon, it was time for chores. Each of us learned to take responsibility for what was assigned to us, but we also developed a sense of pride in the doing. The days melted into one another but not without a sense of being loved, appreciated and cared for.

Attitudes which we develop, already as children, are either growth-fostering or growth-inhibiting. Consider for a moment the presence of a beautiful tree just outside your window. For me, it brings back memories of a time when I was carefree and happy, secure and content in the arms of a loving family. Today, the economy of the world finds little room for seeing and appreciating a thing just as it is in itself. A tree is not just a tree, beautiful, graceful and inviting, holding memories of care-free days. Depending on its species and the business I may be in, it is timber for houses, a source of food, or the newspaper that I pore over at breakfast. People are looked upon in much the same way and labeled as assets or liabilities. We rush past one another in the streets eager to make *our* way, eager to get ahead without acknowledging the mystery, the touch of the Divine that is hidden in the humanness of the other.

What would happen if we committed ourselves to the attitude of 'the respectful look'? Perhaps a little child can help us.

Recently, I observed a small child, perhaps three or four years of age, as she explored a bright, soft, shaggy rug in a local Department store. The throngs of people who hurried past did not intimidate, or distract her in the least. Two small, chubby hands meandered through the soft inviting pile. Then two little cheeks moved up and down testing the softness of the shaggy rug—first the right, then the left in turn. Every so often, a delightful squeal of approval issued from the little one. Though the child may have experienced "rugness" in her own home, it was obvious that she was enjoying this repetition with reinforcing rapture.

I found myself realizing that children have a beautiful way of becoming aware of reality and living in its presence. Repetition for children is relaxing and natural. Repetition, for the child is the seed of the meditative life which is sown in childhood. Have you ever noticed that a child delights in the same story over and over again? The child is able to lose oneself, to go over and over the matter at hand until it is immersed in its realness. I realized that I must put away some of the sophistication which prompts me to look for the ever-new. I need to reconsider some of the things that are so familiar that they have lost their aliveness for me.

In our everyday embeddedness, it seems we have lost the ability for wonder, awe and fascination, and the respectful look and along with it we have been distracted from the reality that life only makes sense in God. These gifts have been snuffed out like candles in the wake of the magic of electricity. Children have a beautiful, sometimes disconcerting, way of becoming aware of reality and living in its presence, but all too soon this, too, is snuffed out by the adult need to 'get on with things'.

The 'Innocent Eye' of a Child

Years ago I was assigned to the care of preschool children in an Orphan Home. One day, just as I was having my mid-day meal of spaghetti and meat-sauce the phone rang in the staff dining room. The message was that the Social Worker had come to take one of the 'baby house' children to the Children's Court and I should hurry and get the child ready. Unaware, in my haste to finish lunch, I managed to drip some spaghetti sauce on the front of my blouse. As I bathed little Keta and tried to hurry the process she refused to cooperate, staring intently at my blouse. I finally said, "Keta, sit down so I can wash your feet." The little one raised her index finger in admonition and said accusingly, "You didn't wear your bib for dinner!"

As I reflected upon the candidness and "accurate" appraisal of this little child, I was led to some thoughtful pondering. How does the mode of my present living make me to be? Am I living in such a 'rush' that it takes on an air of superficiality? Is there a mode of taken-for-grantedness about my life? Am I living in an aura of self deception? How can I make a gift of my life when it is shallow, disparate and lacking focus?

While the incident related above is quite superficial, external, and not at all of a subjective nature, it had a wisdom of the little ones. Her very intent looking and subsequent 'judgment' made me encounter myself. It told me that I must grow in self awareness. I really need the "innocent eye" of the child. A child can stare at an object, a face, examining every aspect or feature of it. She sees the whole as though seeing it for the first time. I need something of the child who does not tire of staring until some "answer" emerges. But often that which is perceived cannot be put into words. Really seeing, means to behold the self that I am, in naked simplicity, never forgetting the 'Ground of my Being'!

With a Loving Look

Attitude, then moves on to center stage! How do I want to see myself? To do this, I must grow in self awareness. Do I merely move linearly through each of my days? What helps me to acknowledge the uniqueness that I really am? Do I see my limitations stacked like cord wood against the winter's cold? Do I see myself as shallow, as empty, as thoughtless, tense or ambitious? If I feel dismayed at the 'unsightliness' I find in myself, I may adopt the attitude of "that's the way I am" so every attempt at change is considered useless. On the other hand, a loving look may already be moving me toward a new vision, a new seeing, and a new determination to be the best I can be. I may resolve to live with heart, longing and will.

Our modern world with all its progress and productivity, gadgets and speed has not served us well in the realm of what Maslow calls 'B-cognition.[1] According to Maslow, B-cognition plays an important role in moments of highest happiness and fulfillment . . . 'peak experiences'. The 'peak-experience' is felt as "a self-validating, self-justifying moment which carries its own intrinsic values in it."[2] It is like a wall plaque which caught my eye recently. It said, in a very artistic way, "Dance, as if you were the only one dancing; sing as if no one heard you and live each day as though it were the best."

B-cognition transcends ordinary awareness, or knowing, in that which is seen or encountered. It is non-comparing, non-evaluating, non-judging. Here a person, or thing, remains with its very own genuine uniqueness. B-cognition facilitates our seeing in greater depth and intensity. Concrete perception of the whole of anything demands sustained attention to it, if it is at all possible. Perception demands a caring, fascinated attending to the thing at hand. It is only in this way that we can hope to come to the richness of detail not visible in mere casual observation, which Maslow says "are the bare bones of experience". [3]

If I truly encounter myself, I find not only limitations, but also potentialities. Acknowledging my limitations and gifts should move me into dialogue with myself and gratitude to the Giver. One quick glance however, at the inner self does not affect a change. What is needed is the repetitious gaze of a child who really wants to know. In wonderment, a child will fix attention on any object. I must take my cue from the child. I must learn to look intently at my attitudes, at the posture I take in regard to events of life, the people whom I encounter and my own self, and also at my relationship with God, the Holy Other. Looking again and again with a loving look will facilitate my coming to the core of my being, to the essence of life—my deepest self.

Making a Shift

It is difficult for me just to be—to bracket all else and to respectfully, meditatively ponder myself just as I am. This takes practice and a rhythm of discipline as I live from day to day. The shift toward quiet acceptance of the self strips me of the external trappings of doing and achieving. It is only in a quiet, guarded space that a shift in my life can take place. This quiet acceptance of self may make me feel alien and lost at first, because it is a new and foreign territory that I am beginning to explore. My destitute condition and self-imposed poverty become quite noticeable to me. But in this caring, loving, repetitious gaze, I learn of a new richness. I begin to see intricate qualities which emerge only after intent searching, seeing with "care". I move from B-cognition to what I like to call *Be-attitude*—a kind of new blessedness. Be-attitude is a giftedness that is mine when I can allow myself to be just as I am, for the moment. Be-attitude is the gracious acceptance of self with all my limitations and faults, supported by the awareness that there is so much good, so much potential in me. Be-attitude is the realization that I am, but that I am also becoming. We do have a treasure in our keeping, but it is of perishable earthenware.

As growth takes place within us, we come to understand more clearly the inadequacy of our own efforts. Undoubtedly, we experience some level of frustration as we come to realize that a good deal of our growth is dependent upon un-learning and employing a Strength beyond ourselves. We are faced with the task of letting go of the tendency to gauge our worth upon externals, accomplishments and the recognition of others. Just as the fourteenth century unknown author of "The Cloud of Unknowing" insisted that it was of highest value to forget some of the 'truths' we fashioned about God, as children, in order to really come to a more authentic realization of who God is for us, so too, we must be willing to forget some of the values and principles regarding self in order to fashion a more holistic, authentic 'me'.

Psychologists tell us that one of the common problems we have to deal with is that of our own self-acceptance.⁴ We come more readily to wholeness when we recognize, and *own*, what fragments and dissipates our lives. Fitting the shards together is a lifetime task, but not an impossible one. It is the work of my becoming and it is the commission that is laid upon each of us at birth. The consoling passage from Ephesians should hearten us. "May you be filled with all the completion God has to give. He whose design is at work in us is powerful enough to carry out his purpose beyond all our hopes and dreams." ⁵ But it requires of us that we remain supple and pliable in the hands of the Divine Potter.

Human beings that we are, sometimes we use a lot of time and energy trying to hide or camouflage our true self. We tend to imagine that others would not "like me" if they really knew me! Maslow says beautifully "that frequently the problems and conflicts of the growth-motivated person are solved by one's self, turning inward in a meditative way, i.e., self-searching rather than seeking help from someone else."[6] Maslow does not mean to say that others cannot help but that I must take the initiative relying on God's grace which is always sufficient for me.

Shedding Expectations

In my careful, meditative self-searching, I find a shedding taking place. I begin to shed the masks I employ to save face, to measure up to what others think of me. I begin to shed my pride. I ask myself, "Is what others think of me really so important?" Slowly I burrow out of the dungeons of my darkness and the hidden truths become so real! I hear myself saying, "Others cannot see my inner core. It is the real me that counts!" I begin to shed my anxiety. I realize that I can never really close the gap between what I am at any given moment and what I am meant to be, except with the help of some very special God-given grace. This is a *crisis* moment. The word 'crisis', coming from the Greek, actually means a point of decision. It is a moment of choice. I can choose to follow the easy path of loitering along or I may opt to embrace the high road of pursuing the goal—wholeness. I shall always be striving, always on the way. I begin to shed impatience. I realize that there is a law of gradualness built into every dimension of my life.

If I pursue my own opinionated will, if I violently try to force my unfolding or refuse to acknowledge the very real situations of my life, I will have to pay the price. Perhaps my becoming will be unbecoming! Being in dialogue with the situation means that I foster a transparency, a readiness to own what reality is really saying to me. I am called to recognize that I am a unity—a body, an ego, and a spirit self. Just as physical growth, for the most part, is slow and imperceptible, so too, is growth on the deeper, spiritual dimension of the self.

The spirit dimension of ourselves must be cared for with the same nurturing awareness with which we attend the needs of the body. We nourish our body with food, sleep, and rhythms of work and recreation. Our spirit also benefits through this 'bodily' care for we are not two entities but body-spirit individuals. However, overemphasis on bodily needs will lead to disaster for the spirit. All must have its time in proper proportions. Just as Scripture tells us there is a time to plant and a time to reap, a time to endure hardships as well as to rejoice, a time to sleep and a time to awake—so there must be a time of 'apartness' for the spirit. Kierkegaard speaks of building nests with one's beloved, but also of the need to have 'time to sit alone on the roof.'[7] We too, need to find a place—a hypothetical roof—where we can slip away from the crowds and the demands of the day, closer to the sky and our Maker.

Growing thus in insightfulness, I am prompted to integrate my life into a project or plan that can help me to realize my deepest self. But no project or plan can materialize without the awareness that God is in control of my life and that it is this Divine Source that nourishes and challenges me through every moment of my existence. Through HIM I experience the 'fire' and 'fuel' that nourishes my every moment.

NOTES:

1. Abraham H. Maslow, Toward a Psychology of Being (Princeton, N.J. D. van Nostand Company, Inc., 1962) p.72.
2. Maslow, Op. Cit., p.74.
3. Ibid.
4. Maslow, Op. Cit., p. 72.
5. Ephesians 3, 19b-20a. (paraphrased)
6. Maslow, Op. Cit., p.35.
7. Soren Kierkegaard, Purity of Heart is to Will One Thing, trans. Douglas Steere (New York: Harper & Row, Publ. 1956) P. 22.

The reader made be interested in pursuing the Beatitudes further in Muto, Susan. Blessings That Make Us Be—A Formative Approach to Living the Beatitudes (Pittsburg, PA Epiphany, Books) 2002.

The current work will deal extensively with the Scriptural Beatitudes in Chapter 13.

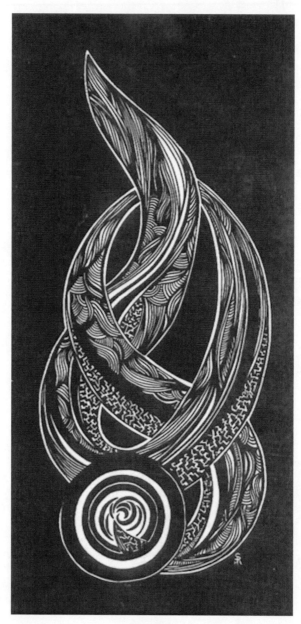

PRAISE

LIVING GOD

Living God
And God of the Living,
You stretch us beyond time,
Giving verdant hope
To by-gone years and seemingly lost moments.

You wrap us in strong faith,
The truth song that gives melody
To darkling mysteries and our faltering dance.

You enfold us in unending love
Melding life's contradictions
Into sculptures of exquisite newness-
Praise pieces to you,
Living God and God of the Living.

FOR REFLECTION:

What seemingly lost moments still haunt me?

Can you name the truth song that gives melody to life's darkling mysteries?

What praise sculptures can you bring to the Living God?

CHAPTER THREE

A TWO-EDGED SWORD

THE QUALITY OF openness to experience is imperative for full, healthy development. The authentic self emerges in a two sided or double edged dimension. I need sufficient managing ability, or ego strength, to be in control, to face what arising situations call for. On the other hand, I must be secure enough to relinquish control. My ego self must not be allowed to dominate me.

Perhaps you remember a carton in which Lucy has to remind Charlie Brown of this. Charlie comes to Lucy's counter which has a sign out in front . . . "PSYCHIATRIC HELP—5 CENTS". Charlie comes to take advantage of this assistance and asks: "What can you do when you don't fit in? What can you do when life seems to be passing you by?" Then Lucy says, "Follow me, I want to show you something." Lucy leads Charlie to a familiar hilltop and she continues: "See that horizon over there. See how big this world is? See how much room there is for everybody? Have you ever seen any other world?" "NO" replies Charlie. "As far as you know this is the only world there is, right?" asks Lucy.

"There are no other worlds to live in . . ." "Right".

"You were born to <u>live</u> in this world . . ." "Right".

"Well, LIVE IN IT, then!" shouts Lucy as she collects her five cents.

Lucy's home-spun 'psychiatry' is no nickel advice! Our entire life in contingent upon the moment by moment unfolding of it, and it is in precisely those moments and in that particular place, where we will meet God or we will not encounter Him at all.

Perhaps you remember that Thoreau went to the woods to live because he wanted to live intently, to seek out the marrow of life's experience and not come to the moment of death and discover that he had never lived.

Thoreau's action hints at the difference between living and being lived. All of human life is lived at the meeting points of the concrete situation in which I find myself and my personal, free response to that situation. My attitude becomes the key to a vibrant existence or one "frittered away".[1]

From birth until death, the self as a dynamic whole is always emerging. This experience of the self, in the process of emerging, unfolds in a variety of experiences which make up the rhythm of daily life. A strong and healthy ego is both a good observer and a good listener. It observes situations that arise, or one may be caught up in, and is able to make a proper, acceptable response. It listens and deals with persons, events and things in a most authentic manner. Proper human growth and becoming is contingent upon the trust I am able to place in my own organism, and in the awareness that a Super-power, the Spirit God, is always with me. My physical, spiritual, emotional self helps me to discover the truth and beauty of each moment—to know that I have only one life to live.

Life—as Celebration

Life is given us to be lived, to be celebrated, to be passionately engaged in! It is in this way that we get to the juices, the marrow of our existence. I can almost hear you saying: "CELEBRATE? You can't keep that up day after day!" The idea of celebration, relative to life, is not new. In the Psalms we have many images of celebration. Not only do people rejoice, but we have images of rivers clapping their hands, of mountains skipping, of hills dancing with joy.

Celebration is not always a formal observance of some kind . . . not an artificial diversion with cocktails and chatter which some would equate with it. Celebration, (even if it is planned) needs to have elements of spontaneity about it. It is genuine rejoicing over something or someone.

Living hinges upon all of life, not just existing, but making of life a "public performance", as it were, with appropriate rituals, keeping always in mind that life is a gift we honor with a grateful and happy satisfaction. Celebration is singing to our very existence and at the same time affirming our Creator. True celebration needs to be re-creative, and fulfilling.

In celebrating we look to the Lord with radiant joy. Life's victories and passages invite us to celebrate. We come to appreciate the richness of living, the dignity of work, the sense of fulfillment and accomplishment. What appropriate rituals do we need to recognize?

Our ancient world was attuned to myriad rites. The rite of Spring, for instance, rites centering around family, community, the rites of passage marking a person's progress from one state or level to the next. Some cultures and countries still hold ritual ceremonies which mark crossing over. In the Mexican culture, the "Quinsinera años" is truly such a rite. This celebrates the passage of a fifteen year old female youth into womanhood and it is marked with great festivity, color and often cost. It is a celebration in ritual but it also is the celebration of an event. This girl has reached her fifteenth birthday! It is an accomplishment. It is a cause to celebrate!

For nearly ten years I was privileged to work in Kenya. The customs and culture are quite different from our own, but meaningful in their own way. My development and administration of an elementary school allowed me to become familiar with customs, culture and various religious practices. One of these was the rite of circumcision.

When a lad completes Grammar school he is ready for the rite of passage. This takes the form of circumcision. The lads who have completed primary school undergo this rite before entrance into Secondary. It is a very special ritual. Boys of the proper age and circumstance are brought together for this 'religious' experience. They are secluded for some fourteen days, or more, after the simple operation. During this span of time only the Priests, Ministers, Elders, the Doctor and Chief of the village may visit them. Even their meals must be catered in by a male chef. During this seclusion they are instructed every day on proper adult behavior, the dignity of sex, honor to their country and the importance of being grateful to God for their existence. Daily prayer time is woven into this seclusion. Literally, the boys are transformed when they return to 'society'.

As the seclusion reaches its end, each one of the lads must be completely outfitted with new clothes. The symbolism is that this young man has taken on a new identity. Then the festival begins and all well wishers, parents and significant others join in the celebration which usually concludes with some form of worship, Mass or prayer vigil.

We become what we celebrate. Our consumer oriented society with its economics, instant relief from any and all illness or discomfort, wants to make us believe that this is living as its best! Economic, political and social valuing come together and point uniformly to one problem—loss of identity and insipid living. While life has something of the product mentality about it, getting stuck in particulars of persons, places and events of life vitiate against the process of becoming. Though we make strides in taming nature, conquering the realm of space and improving living conditions there is still an uneasiness and bewilderment that permeates many lives. Persons often experience themselves as a commodity. I am led to believe that if I am successful in business, and the daily trafficking of life, I am valuable; if I fail to amass wealth and fame, I am worthless. The treacherous thing, in extrinsic valuing, is that a person is at the mercy of the system. Society sets the standards and I must conform. I become the pawn of the fickle and competitive market. The ever-changing, fluidity of the economic and socio-political world conjures up flimsy standards for celebrating life.

These very standards deprive me of a sense of security. This triumvirate of power (economic, social, and political) however, is for a great majority of people their only yardstick of success as well as the only affirmation they expect. Estrangement and despondency often ensue. This very issue is the reason for many marriages today to fall apart. If love is not greater than the triple-tiered 'monarch' a relationship cannot last. With great imagery Erich Fromm describes this state of a person estranged from self. He uses a literary analogy. In _Peer Gynt_, the character by the name of Ibsen who is living an estranged state of selfhood tries to discover his authentic self. He finds however, that he is like an onion—one layer after another is peeled away with no core to be found.[2] The core of one's self is in finding one's true worth. It is in recognizing that I am unique, created and loved by God. Because of this spiritual quality, we remind ourselves of the power which lies within each individual person to deform or transform, to disfigure or transfigure one's self. We can rise from the dingiest clot of clay to the fairest of creatures. The attitudes which I form already early in life influence the way I meet life's daily situations. If I am living from the center, my response will be one of gratitude to God and grateful rejoicing for the gift that I am and for the fact that God has called me 'friend'. "I call you friends since I have made known to you all that I heard from the Father." (Jn. 15:15)

Pursuing my Identity

Fromm believes that every person should try to become more responsive to the world in which one lives. He believes that we must leave behind the narrow confines of the ego and all its ambitious pride and reach out to that which presents itself—a person, a flower, a book or an idea. Fromm continues saying that since persons cannot exist doubting their identity they borrow from the marketing world and fix their opinion of themselves relative to power, status, or success. Then they become utterly dependent on the way others look at them. This becomes a substitute for a genuine feeling of identity.[3]

As the world sees it, whatever is unique or truly individual in me is useless, against the norms of power, productivity and wealth, but the truth is that my individuality and uniqueness as I come from the hand of God is that which I should celebrate! We are caught up in a world of conformity. We simply cease to be ourselves. Thus cast into a mold, we adopt the patterns and standards of the world around us and we conveniently disappear into the collectivity. Recently I came across a very old book. Pages brittle and yellow with age tell the story of one who refused to be swept along with the current tides of wealth, success and personal gain. Published in 1909, *The Wanamaker Primer on Abraham Lincoln* is composed of annals of Abe's honesty, uprightness, charity, compassion and respect for God and the dignity of every person no matter the race, and of creation. Lincoln did not appear to have one ounce of human respect in his character. He stood for what was right and just beyond all odds. Even as President of the United States when men of his Cabinet mocked and belittled him, he bore their taunts because he recognized the good that each could do for his country. He held no grudges. One of the short sayings of Lincoln has come down to us: "A man has no time to spend in quarrels. If any man ceases to attack me, I never remember the past against him." It seems Lincoln could see the good in another regardless of the way that person treated him. Is it any wonder that, even to this day, we list Mr. Lincoln as one of the great personages of our United States?

Fromm compares the pseudo-value existence of indecisive, vacillating people to the characteristic of protective coloration which is the gift of some animals and created species.[4] Persons become so like the environment they live in, that they lose their individual identity. This happens in religious communities, too! We take on so much of the world, its standards, values and mannerisms that dedicated life loses its identity and uniqueness, and its appeal.

The world that we live in calls us to look outward, to grasp the momentary relief, to 'celebrate' the ephemeral and passing things of life. Then at the deeper core of our being, we are still restless, empty and hollow. It causes a search for meaning through a warped pampering of the self. Recreation, food, individual pursuits of business and ever-widening circles of independence replace the Holy Ground within. We are beings of body, soul and spirit. We are called to look inward, to lasting values and spiritual realities. Bodily comforts and satisfactions cannot satisfy the WHOLE person. Naturally, a struggle ensues. What do I allow to dominate in my life? Do I fail to recognize that without God, I am risking utter failure?

Activity and productivity are qualities that society approves. The passion for involvement all around us often generates a rush of premature, sometimes futile, activity. It's almost like keeping an empty pot on the stove at full boil. Nothing comes of it but a melted base, frayed edges and a charcoal-colored, useless pot. Nothing at all to celebrate!

When God gifts us with life, there are three networks that play out their role with each person. It is in the realm of these networks that we can live out another category of celebration, which is to demonstrate grateful and happy satisfaction for life, its development and the Gift.

The first of these networks is wholly interior to each person. The second is a network of relationships and the third is a network with created things. The first network hinges upon the question: "What is this mysterious Core or Center within me toward which all that I am, and all that I can yet be, gravitates?" In pondering this question, I come to encounter the spiritual depth within myself which tells me plainly that I am more than my body and all the bodily pleasures that I pursue to satisfy it. When I come to that fundamental realization an intrinsic value surfaces!

Patka refers to this fundamental value as 'religious value' which he says is the foundation of all value categories. It is, also, the basic premise of this writing. All perfection and progress of the world is meaningful only if it is put into the proper perspective as regards the Source of its origin. Patka contends that our erratic thinking, consequent upon technological strides, has robbed us "of faith in the Absolute" thereby causing us to lose faith in ourselves, humankind and our own personal endeavors.[5] When we give it some deep and intense thought, progress is not progress at all when it minimizes the good of humankind and disregards the dignity of the person.

Whether we have come to the point of acknowledgement, or not, the Holy Other is pivotal. God is the "still point" of each 'lifetime burning in every moment'[6]. The awareness that God is with us, accompanies us and knows our inmost being, sustains us. There are several radical assumptions (or truths) which underpin this reality. The first is that human beings do not find God through a reasoning process. God is MYSTERY and this involves an entirely different approach. Mystery is a matter of the heart and as the Fox tells the Little Prince, "It is only with the heart that one can see rightly; what is essential is invisible to the eye."[7] God is so much greater than any power of our own. It is God Himself who invites us into a personal relationship through which we begin to 'feel' God's love and bask in the sunshine of it. It is necessary that we let ourselves be immersed in that love and foster conditions that nurture it.

The fundamental or intrinsic assumption in a person's search for self is ultimately a searching for God who is invisible! In reflecting upon and accepting our creature-hood we, in the same instance, acknowledge our Creator. The only course open to us after this is what Gabriel Marcel, the French, Catholic existentialist philosopher referred to, as "creative fidelity".[8]

The Pursuit of Transcendence

Creative fidelity is opposed to both a fantastic notion of freedom as well as conformism. Freedom does not exist for its own sake, but as a means for a person's fuller participation in 'being'. Marcel reasons that freedom is a framework in which a person determines, independently, the manner of response of each person to life. It is a person's prerogative to witness to the transcendent or to repudiate it. Marcel's concept of freedom is supported by an ontological humility, i.e., recognition of our finite creatureliness.

In the stance of fidelity we are able to rise above moments of "life-flux" and pledge loyalty to the Transcendent God. Herein, we acknowledge our own finiteness and inferiority. The false gods of self-sufficiency, power, fame and riches must be dethroned. The gods of science, technology, art and music are unable to redeem humankind!

Along with fidelity, we consider the allied virtues of hope and love. Marcel describes hope paradoxically as the "weapon of the unarmed"[9] Hope operates as a technique, or power, enabling one to overcome difficulties in the pursuit of transcendence. "Reflecting on hope is perhaps our most direct meaning of the word transcendence, for hope is a spring, a leaping of a gulf."[10] A person imbued with hope moves upward and onward. It enables the person to spring over the obstacles that thwart progress toward authentic personhood. Hope implies a kind of refusal to pay attention to seeming impossibilities and to "touch a principle in the heart of things, or rather in the heart of events, which mock such reckonings."[11] Hope is not a call to escape or inactivity. It is a very human response which activates one in the presence of helplessness or inability.

The opposite of hope, pessimism, is rooted in the same soil as despair. This contributes largely to becoming more and more self-centered, thus decreasing the possibility of celebrating life and of being available for others. Then the development of the second network, the network of relationships, is stymied. Marcel warns against ego-centrism. So does our Lord! Hospitality and welcoming others puts the axe to inordinate attention of self. We need to nourish a climate of the heart as did Jesus throughout Scripture. Jesus is hospitality personified. Jesus was forever reaching out to restore life, to heal, to nourish. He gave of Himself fully, unreservedly, even to death. I have lived with persons who fear the unknown, who are reluctant to move beyond proven comfort, or to risk dependable security. All of this turns people inward, rather than outward. Their horizons telescope in on themselves. Egocentricity negates genuine hospitality and it is best overcome through compassion for others because compassion makes me sensitive to the needs of others. The time and attention I give to another is bound up with the giving of self. In Jesus' death we see this giving played out beyond measure.

Marcel's reflections on love are fragmentary but conducive to meaningful insights. He believes that one who is incarcerated within the confines of his own ego-centric prison cannot really be a person. Marcel offers a statement about the authenticity of love. True love, he says, is defined in the proportion as I love less for my own sake, and more for the sake of the other. He may have come to this definition pondering the example of the total self-giving of Jesus as He offered himself unreservedly for our salvation. Jesus definitely could not say to the Father, "What do I get out of it?" or "What's in it for me?"

Love also finds its expression in availability. This availability demands involvement at least in the interest of the other. Remember that Jesus told us, 'what you do for the least, you have done for Me?' People automatically respond to this love and it is the quiet process of making another 'be'. We are consciously or unconsciously involved in the formation of others. We enter the realm of co-existence. We are beings-through-others an no one goes the way alone!

Encounter: Finding God in Others

As I worked in a remote village in Kenya, because we did not own a vehicle, I used to walk up to the "mutatu" stage to board a sort of public taxi which ferreted people back and forth to larger towns for medical appointments, shopping, banking and sundry purposes. To shorten the distance I most always ventured though the market area—even when the Saturday and Tuesday produce was not available. Without fail, I would see a large group of boys, emaciated and dirty, but ever so friendly and smiling, digging through the refuse for food scraps to share among themselves. It was both edifying and heartbreaking to see them share a crumpled, dirty cabbage leaf with one another. Tearing it in pieces, each boy got a 'bite'. They looked too, for plastics and metals which they could sell for a few shillings. It was my way to greet them, speak a few words in their dialect, Kimeru, and then continue on my way.

After some months and having become 'friends', a cordon of Boys of various ages, lined up in front of me and chorused in their labored English, to be sure I would understand, "Sister! We want to go to school!" For the moment, I was startled, but I promised them I would see to it.

Now this was no small matter because these Boys were living on the Street. No place to take a bath, no 'real' food, no one to get admission for them to school and to come up with the required school fees, uniforms, shoes etc. But the biggest challenge was to find a Home for the Boys where they could bathe, sleep, eat and have a sense of belonging and dignity. All the way to town and back, the Boys' chorus haunted me.

The first chance I had, I approached some people with 'authority' about the village and asked "What are we doing about the many Boys living on the Streets in the Market area?" A little stunned at the question, the reply was slow in coming: "Well that really is the Government's problem," and that was the end of the conversation.

Thoughts of the Boys obsessed me during the day and into the sleeping hours. I knew I must do something. There was not enough money available to build a home for the Boys so, initially, I resorted to the idea of renting a place. I recruited several of my trusted workers to help me in the search. Before long, the men came back and reported that they had found a large vacant store front that could accommodate approximately twenty or more boys. This would not address the need totally, but it would be a beginning. We were all very happy and enthusiastic! However, our euphoria was soon to be dashed to the ground. As it often occurs in villages, someone of means, usually a business man, from a distant town or city owns the property which may have ten or twelve rooms located in back of the store-front. These one-room "row" dwellings are rented out to families just barely providing a roof over their heads. Cooking is done over an open fire in the court yard and bathing and toilet facilities are shared by all.

When the news 'broke' that I wanted to rent the store front for Street Boys, there was instant protest. "We will have to share our facilities with these dirty kids! Our kids won't be safe!! What will we be getting into?" Consequently, the good Christian owner would not rent to me for fear of losing his patrons.

Yes, we were disheartened, but we did not give up. At this point, I must confess, that the men had more faith than I did. "We'll keep looking!" they said, "There has to be something available." Not many days hence they returned triumphantly and exclaimed, "We have found the ideal place! No one will bother us!" Eager to see this wonderful find, I mobilized myself immediately.

The location was good, just off the main market area on a side street. To my dismay, the place was a disaster! It was an abandoned slaughter house and it seemed to me beyond repair or possible use. The men immediately picked up my consternation and assured me that they could salvage it. Still, I was doubtful! But they went to work! Because the place had been vacant for a long time there was no animal stench. That was about the only 'plus' I could initially hang on to. There was no electricity, no source of water and the place was miserably uninviting. Walls were painted a deep red about six feet from the floor, and everywhere there was trash galore; refuse of indescribable origin, filth and rubbish accumulation. One room up front, that had served as a sort of "kiosk" or 'hotel' in the native mentality, seemed the only remote possibility. Off of this room was a dingy two by four kitchen with an open fireplace and behind it an empty wood shed which boasted in scrawled letters "Free for Sex". "Oh" I thought, "if we take over this place, we will close that den of iniquity!"

I cannot give enough credit to the workers who shoveled out cart loads of rubbish, scrubbed and painted until the place was transformed. My handy maintenance man installed a solar panel for light, dug latrines in what had been the holding yard for the animals before slaughter, constructed cubicles for bathing and gave the entire place an air of respectability. Water was still missing, so I courageously approached the Water Department for assistance. They provided us with one tap but it would have to do. I went to town again and bought a supply of plastic buckets which we could dole out to the kids and for use in the small kitchen.

Despite all our efforts only a handful of Boys could be accommodated. The only useable room for sleeping, (even with a thin mattress on the floor), eating, study, socializing—for everything—was the former 'hotel' room. Without advertising, we opened up on a 'first come' basis and filled the available space in less than ten minutes. What a joy on the one hand and what sheer disappointment on the other! Many tears flowed that evening while the hopes of deserving young lads were shattered.

The fifteen Boys we were able to accommodate, responded beautifully to the attention that was shown them. After a 'taming' period in which they needed to be weaned from glue bottles, independent living and no schedule at all in their lives, the Boys became a disciplined 'wonder' to all in the village. They truly enjoyed the challenge of the classroom and excelled in studies. It was a 'mustard seed' beginning, but God blessed the endeavor and gave the increase. Even as I write, I had a message from the currently "in-charge" that one of the Boys managed 600 points, out of 600, on his last exam. The Boys put their heart and soul into everything!

Love as Presence

These kids in their previous existence, as well as those who could not be accommodated that first evening, serve as a good example of negative presence. All the people in the area were aware of these Boys living on the Street, but the Boys existed only in a juxta-position to them. The Boys were there but "not there". As long as this condition exists it is only possible to achieve a kind of physical 'presence' to one another but love, care and compassion are out of the question. Eventually, we were able to build a residence for the Boys that were left. The lucky ones from the "slaughterhouse" joined them for a happy reunion. Now they all live in a well-deserved "Caring Place".

"Presence is that inward realization, through love, of an immediacy."[11] It is not proximity or spatial relationships which form the substratum of presence, but rather a mutual oneness _with_ the other as being to being. "With" connotes a precise form of response, some degree of possibility or interiority, of identifying our being with that of another, in a kind of reciprocity . . . not a subject-object relationship.[12] Marcel speaks of presence as something which is immediately visible in a handshake, a smile, a look, in listening. He reflects on a way of listening which is a way of giving life and of another way of listening which is a way of refusal . . . of refusing the gift of one's self. Listening has many dimensions. I may hear the chirping of the birds, but not necessarily listen to them. I may hear the cry of a child, but ignore it for anyone of myriad reasons. On the other hand I may give the child my attention and sooth the discomfort, fear or loneliness.

When others are encountered as person, the 'other' passes from the impersonal realm of "it" to the personal realm of "thou". It is in this instance that my own personal being emerges, and I am aware of being situated in this world. Being with others is a dimension of my world and how often our world is too small!

Unless I grace a person or a situation with my personal presence love remains barren and empty. Actually, it is not love at all! The true reaching out to another in need, affirms my graced humanness. Ignoring the need of another is not mere passivity; it is more than that. It is self-alienation which deprives me of acquiring knowledge of myself. We must never forget that it is love which enables me to give without diminishing the gift. The self is the essence of the gift and God is the Giver. We, as followers of Christ, are challenged to be persons of love, caring and compassionate. Jesus was our Model. Did He not say "Learn of Me?"

Cathedral of Creation

We have yet to consider the network of created things. Nature in general—birds, flowers and trees—the vastness of blue skies, sunsets and bees ought to hold a fascination for us. Each bears an imprint of the Creator's hand. I learned to love the starry heavens through the eyes of my father. Sometimes in the long summer days, when indoors was sweltering (air-conditioning was yet to be invented) we waited outdoors in the inviting breeze for darkness to fall and for the house to cool. These were precious times of encounter with mother and dad who shared stories of the day and of life experiences.

As the first stars began to appear, Dad often drew our attention to the heavens. After sometime he would point out various constellations: "Look there is Orion. That big 'M' is Cassiopeia, and there is the Milky Way . . ." Dad used to tell us, as kids, about one constellation we would never see because we lived in the northern hemisphere. His description of it was so clear that I recognized it immediately, years later as I observed it both in Asia and Africa. "That one", he would say, "looks like a perfect cross and sometimes in the early evening you will find it close to the horizon". To this day, I relish a starry night and the Southern Cross is always a reminder to me of my father's knowledge and reverence for creation.

The unlimited diversity of earth's landscape invites reflective wonder and wondering refection. Plains, mountains, plateaus and rivers cover the face of the earth. Consider the monochromatic expanses of the Nevada desert, or the jagged, great peaks of the Rockies covered with tinges of snow in the morning sunlight. Across continents we can observe the same beauty as the sun etches out the magnificent Alps, the Himalayas or the stalwart Mt. Kenya. See the waving far-reaching fields of Kansas grain or the flaming contrast of an autumnal hillside in peaceful Vermont. Behold in your minds' eye the less beautiful, but captivating, pockmarked and wrinkled appearances of Death Valley, or the tattered, arid lands of Utah. All connote a "having-lived though" time and space and the wisdom and love of the Creator.

The characteristic 'responsiveness'[13] of a creature distinguishes a living organism from a dead one. It is a prerogative of every living creature to respond to stimuli in one way or other. As one proceeds up the ladder of living things, we come to the level of humankind whose responsiveness is remarkably different from that of the lower forms of creation. In the plant or animal kingdom, everyone of a given species responds in an identical way. Plants send roots downward into the soil or into some substitute medium. Animals respond to instinct such that we might say a cat is a cat is a cat. Every creature on earth has a 'life' of its own. We, however, are the only creatures who can lift up heart and soul to the Creator in gratitude and wonder. The gamut of responses is so diverse that each individual is able to respond in a unique way. One praises God in words, another in song and dance, yet another in quiet awe. In reverent gratitude we celebrate the goodness of God.

I cannot any longer remember the exact source, but I find it again and again in my jot book of favorite quotes. It is attributed to Meister Eckhart. In speaking of the Incarnation, Christ's becoming Emmanuel, and taking on our nature, he exclaimed, "If this birth has truly taken place within you, then every single creature points you toward God." O, would that we could live in such intimacy and awareness.

NOTES:

1. Henry David Thoreau, <u>Walden</u>, (Boston: Houghton, Mifflin Co.,1957), p.62.
2. Erich Fromm, <u>Man For Himself</u> (New York Rhinehart and Company, Inc., 1949), p. 73.
3. <u>Ibid</u>
4. Erich Fromm, <u>Escape From Freedom</u> (New York: Holt, Rinehart and Wiston, 1941), p.18
5. Frederick Patka, <u>Values and Existence: Studies in Philosophical Anthropology</u> (New York: Philosophical Library, 1964) p.28.
6. T.S. Eliot, <u>The Complete Poems and Plays 1909-1950</u> (N.Y.: Harcourt, Brace and World, Inc. 1958) p. 129
7. Antoine de Exupèry, <u>The Little Prince</u> (New York: Harcourt Brace and World,1943), p 87.
8. James Collins, <u>The Existentialists—A Critique Study</u> (Chicago: Henry Regnery, Co., 1952) p. 162.
9. Gabriel Marcel, <u>Being and Having</u>, trans. Katherine Farrar (New York: Harper & Row Publishers, 1949), p.76.
10. <u>Ibid.</u>, p. 79.
11. Gabriel Marcel. <u>The Philosophy of Existentialism</u>, trans. Manya Harari (New York: The Citadel Press, 1964), p.15.
12. Gabriel Marcel. <u>The Mystery of Being II, Faith and Fidelity</u>, trans. Rene Hague (Chicago: Henry Regnery Co., 1951), p. 218.
13. Brian Hocking. <u>Biography or Oblivion</u> (Cambridge, MASS.: Schenkman Publ. Co., Inc., 1965) p. 12.

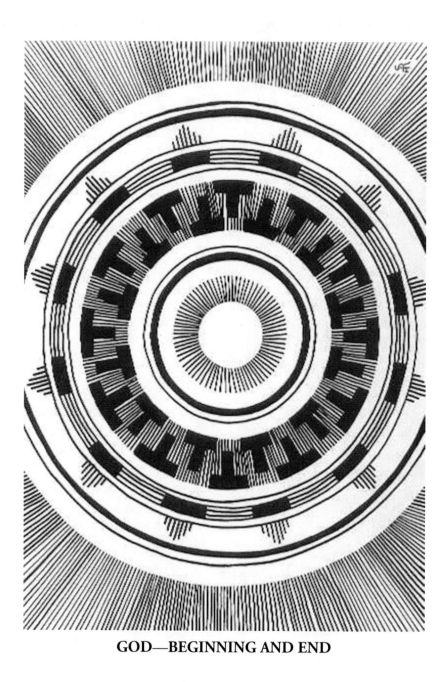

GOD—BEGINNING AND END

AWARENESS-SILENT FIRE

God, Ground of my Being!
Breathe of my life
Why all the struggle and endless strife
To be in your presence—
When in reality,
Without your presence,
I would not be!

I spend my day—quite unaware,
That God is present everywhere.
I've no existence apart from the One
Whose nearness is
As fire to the Sun!

FOR REFLECTION:

When have I experienced God as the Ground of my Being?

What keeps me from recognizing God's nearness?

In my deepest Self, do I really believe that my existence depends on God?

CHAPTER FOUR

QUESTIONS AND THE QUEST

IN HIS SUBTLY humorous way G.K. Chesterton makes a poignant observation about life. He says that when he starts out on the journey of life, he often gets distracted by 'an entertaining lamp-post or a vividly signaling window-blind'. What seems to disturb him most is his inability to size up the measure of difference between the unimportant questions and the Quest, itself. [1]

With birth, I am ushered into the journey of life, enroute as it were toward a great Quest—not as knight-errants of old in search of adventure, treasure or the Holy Grail—but in search of self-hood.

Throughout life, my being is entrusted to me as summons. I must decide what I am to be and become fully what I am—a human being.[2] Life places me in a tension between the temporal and the spiritual. The vital-functional-spiritual synthesis that I am establishes me in a rhythm of being and becoming: past and present, present and future, life and death. Always a dynamic parallelism exists sequestering both questions and Quest within the myriad folds of daily living. Side by side with this reality is the risk for each of us that "an entertaining lamp-post or vividly signaling window-blind" may distract us from our goal.

The fact that *I am* is readily recognizable. The fact that *I am becoming* is less convincing because it is never a completely finished phenomenon. The Quest—the search for self is the goal of life. We are caught up in the process through the art of our living. This is the movement toward self-actualization. Erich Fromm expresses this thought when he writes that the two cells which gave us life, culminate in death. In between these two points, the development of the self must take place out of the 'stuff' of my givenness. Try as we might, we never quite reach the goal since it is the propensity of human nature to 'die before[one is] fully born'. [3]

Maturation consists in following the plan contained in my initial 'givenness', even as it came from the hand of the Divine Source, Herein, I strive to effect the realization of my deepest originality. The Quest for wholeness and holiness is often vaguely defined against the backdrop of life, growth and maturation. The pursuit is often obscured or side-tracked in our functionalistic world! We are forever distracted with "doing and accomplishment" on such mundane levels that we feel ourselves like robots or machines. We become absorbed in accomplishment! The residue of this is that persons around us become "doings' rather than beings. Caught in the prison of the workaholic, I am unfree to pursue the quest of the "more than" which life has to offer.

Thanks to our Creator despite obstacles and distractions along the way, the persistent search for self is motivated from within. It is an urge nestled in the deepest center of every individual. No matter what, we pursue a search for meaning though the search may take circuitous paths and unwelcome detours along the way. We experience a growing hunger and an insatiable thirst to bring to life all that was potentially given me at conception.

Self as Meaning-giver

Central to an individual's quest for selfhood is the characteristic of one's essence referred to as meaning-giver. Heidegger refers to this essential characteristic as "lumen naturale." He suggests that we are beings who ourselves shed light. We uncover meaning only through encountering someone or something in our world.[4]

A personal example may help to clarify this principle. Some years ago I was privileged to minister in the charming, fascinating world of India. Daily, I became more conscious of myself in a world of vendors, sellers and hawkers bargaining on the streets to sell their wares. Some items were unfamiliar to me, and therefore meaningless. I recall even now, the sound of the vendor's cry—or so it sounded to me. "Ootiappl, ootiappl!" It said nothing to me regarding his wares, but the persistent, sustained call spoke to me of another meaning: "BUY, PURCHASE MY WARES! SUPPORT MY FAMILY!" Because my curiosity got the better of me, I went to the window and leaned far out to get a glimpse of the contents of the basket that was balanced gracefully upon the vendor's head. I smiled to myself as I recognized the plump red plums. "Ootiappl" had become meaningful to me. Empathetically, I entered the world of the vendor as I purchased some of the plums and assisted the vendor to earn a living. The darkness which confronted me at that sound of "Ootiappl" was dispelled by the ability I had to confer 'light"/meaning.

This is an example on a purely human level. But we, as graced individuals, can find meaning and confer light upon 'deeper issues'. Why does someone of the status of Mother Teresa of Calcutta go for years feeling dry, desolate and bereft of God's presence? God Alone holds the answer, but we find meaning, as did Mother Teresa, in quiet acquiescence to God's will. It was here that she found peace and the strength to bear the cross that was laid upon her. It was the 'light' she needed.

Individuals are also revealed to themselves though moods. Moods are modes which make it possible for persons to concern themselves with others, with things and with themselves in their world. The simple narrative above attests to this. As I progressed from a curious mode to an "enlightened" one, I found myself sincerely sympathetic with the vendor who tried to eke out a living for himself and his family.

Mood tells us something about the way we interact with other people and informs us as to our situation among things. Our primordial mood is the awareness of the fact that *I am.* I am not merely a 'body' in a given '*world*', I am the beloved of God the Creator. Further reflection leads me to recognize a mood of fundamental affirmation, perhaps a stable mood of resignation or ideally, a mood celebration of life which takes the mode of joyful thanksgiving for each moment allotted to me. However, an event or a series of events may swing a joyful mood into one of despondency, depression or even silent desperation. Of themselves, events of life are neither good nor bad, nor are they capable of causing us to wallow in negative responses. Events become cloaked in their negative, undesirable nuance because of my mood and the meaning I bestow upon them, or vice versa.

We begin to see that the call to selfhood is an ongoing summons and that the Quest is a continuing search. Adrian van Kaam says that there are

M. GERMAINE HUSTEDDE, PHJC

two basic postures of response in our searching, namely the playful mode of existence, or the mode of reality called labor.[5] The playful aspect of life enables us to leave behind daily tasks, worries and preoccupations and to be committed to a type of activity that hinges upon play and festivity. We engage in life in a more carefree world of celebration. Everyday life, however, calls us to a mode of reality which we define as labor. This is experienced as a mode of commitment to some activity which is linked to practical aims and utilitarian projects. While there is truth in the reality, that we need labor for our daily bread, for a just wage, and sustenance, we often go overboard and all but idolize work such that it claims all my waking hours and even the Sabbath.

We could look upon these two modes of existence, the playful and labor oriented, as stretching along a continuum. At the middle of the personality field the most mature and well balanced individuals cluster. At either end of the continuum and scattered somewhere in between the midpoint, are the individuals who tend toward either playfulness or mastery. In some persons the tendency to receptivity prevails while in others the bent for mastery dominates. van Kaam says that persons who tend to be less efficient in the area of mastery are by nature more contemplative and receptive. The blessing of this bent is that such persons experience life more as 'presence' while those given to mastery and work view life as a 'challenge'[6]

Persons who are prone to mastery experience the world as responsibility linked to practical aims. There is a sense of "Today, I have to accomplish this . . ." When the goal is not reached, there is a nagging feeling of guilt or disappointment at least. This person feels most rewarded when practically engaged in some measureable activity.

A person's individual stance regarding the modes of receptivity and mastery are difficult to determine precisely. However, in thoughtful, reflective moments I can ascertain whether I tend to be more like the "busy-about-many-things" Martha of the Gospels or whether I am more prone to quiet presence. Martha seemingly depicts a person with a high propensity toward mastery while Mary portrays a rewarding capacity for receptivity and contemplation.[7]

The old timeless adage seems very applicable here. "All work and no play makes Jack a dull boy!" We conclude that the most mature and balanced individual seems to be the one who has achieved a noble blending of the two modes of existence, work and play. But, we know too, that such a perfect blending of receptivity and mastery is the ideal, a rare occurrence indeed. It remains for us to be sensitive to our given propensity and take measures to discipline ourselves toward achieving a life-giving balance.

Practicing the Art

The quest for genuine selfhood and growth into personal mastery is an art. One of the requirements of the art is that I possess a willingness to be a process rather than a product. Skill in any art is achieved only by long, arduous and persistent practice. However, if I aim at fixed goals and stress the notion of product mentality, I am forever setting boundaries for myself. My life becomes one big ego project. Instead of building bridges, I build fences and erect walls. While life has something of the product mentality about it, getting stuck in particulars of persons, places and things vitiate against the process of becoming.

Contrariwise, we can emphasize the spiritual dimension of self such that we can rise from the dingiest clot of clay to the fairest of creatures. I perceive all of my striving against the backdrop of the Holy Who sustains and cares for me as well as all those with whom I come in contact. The horizon of the Whole and the Holy becomes the dayspring of my life and the sustaining force in my Quest.

In his book, *The Art of Loving*, Fromm lists four general requirements necessary for the practice of any art: discipline, concentration, patience, and supreme concern.[8] Without *discipline*, I shall never be adept at anything. I need to approach a desired goal in a disciplined way. If fitful moods or vacillating feelings propel me, I will never become a master at what I am trying to achieve. My heart must be in it in the first place!

Discipline is a rather personal need and it will be experienced differently by each of us. It is a means of helping us to overcome the things that clutter our lives and get in the way of our safe journeying. Discipline clears the path of the proverbial stumbling blocks. It helps us to become integrated—to come to wholeness.

Discipline is not a part-time affair. It involves the whole of life. Though our lives are governed by a certain amount of work-associated regulations there is nevertheless too little self-imposed discipline. We react strongly to the routines of life and authority imposed by the structure of cultural and daily living. We want to "relax"! Fromm says that this description is merely a more refined way of saying that we are "lazy". This attitude toward discipline renders the Quest for selfhood fragmented and chaotic. It presupposes that there can be no element of concentration in my life.

Fromm maintains that *concentration* in the western culture is even more rare than self-discipline. It shows up in our diffuse and scattered way of life. We are bombarded from every side to use every waking moment in activity, dialogue and such. Ready access to cell phones, email, internet and iPod keep us in perpetual motion and 'worldly' noise is a "must". The radio and TV go from morning to night even when no one is listening. I recall an incident from ages ago when I was still involved in education. Class VIII was having a final Math Exam. I observed one of the boys fidgeting, visibly uncomfortable. I quietly approached him and asked, "What is troubling you?" He looked at me in all seriousness and said, "Sister, it is so quiet in here I can't think!"

We are prone to do a host of things at one time. We are reluctant to sit still, to be alone or to welcome quiet. We become ever more nervous and fidgety. The self is always divided. The admonition of the Psalmist is lost on us. "Be still and know that I am God."(Ps. 46:10) We are not being asked to refrain from speech. More so, we are being advised to rest in the Lord, to quiet our inner self and to keep our eyes and hearts fixed on the goal of coming to a deeper, more intense awareness of who I am before God and in God. This is the ultimate goal of my Quest.

The third factor which we are to consider is that of *patience.* Patience is the antipode of instant results or intolerance. Impulsiveness and superficiality are trademarks of persons who are too impromptu to savor life. We live in a NOW generation! If I cannot see immediate results the product is "no good, the therapy is taking just too long, I just can't invest all this time . . ." Often our attitude toward life negates the possibility of developing patience as an art, since the practice of any art is slow, deliberate and ongoing.

In addition, the mastery of any art demands that it be of *ultimate concern* to me. If a goal is of minor or secondary importance, I will never put my utmost energy into achieving it. If I have little concern in pursuing the Quest for selfhood, authentic becoming will be lost in a myriad of lesser values.

Stages of Life/ Indian Perspective

Interestingly, similar to Fromm's components of the art of living, are the Indian stages of life which are based on the requirements of human nature.[9] In this Eastern similitude, we find another way of growing into genuine selfhood. Just as the day has waxing and waning of light, our life, too, has waxing and waning of bodily powers. This reality underlies the theory of the four stages.

The movements defined in a person's life within the Indian context are *bramacharya,* the period of discipline in education, *garhasthya,* the period of the world's work, *vanaprasthya,* retreat for the loosening of bonds; and finally *pravrajya,* the expectant waiting for freedom toward death. The goal of the first stage, bramacharya, is not merely learning from books, or even through experience. The chief lesson of this first stage is a disciplined training of the will so that both enjoyment and renunciation come with equal ease. According to this philosophy, life for many is a pilgrimage ending in complete liberation. Therefore the whole of life is looked upon as a spiritual exercise and must be carried through the subsequent stages with vigilance and reverence.

After the initial training in discipline comes the second stage of life's development known as the life of the house-holder, (my house) or the world's work, garhasthya. The Indian culture holds that once a person looses touch with life, one can no longer approach discipline effectively. Tagore commented that wisdom does not attain completeness except through the living of life. Discipline that is divorced from wisdom is stupidity and possibly meaningless adherence to custom, to quick fixes, or to fads. Through 'work', a decline of our natural stamina is effected. Thus, the physical change should signal to me that I am approaching my twilight years. As bodily powers wane and vigor declines it is a proclamation of a new growth toward freedom. It is to be accepted joyfully as a sign of maturation!

Now I pass into the stage of vanaprasthya! I can be aloof from the world, though not out of touch with it. There is still an interchange between self and the world, but the intimate, dependent exchange that is characteristic of the householder is lacking. An intensified degree of distance and detachment results.

In the fourth stage, pravrajya, the soul is freed. Tagore expresses it this way: "The emancipated soul steps out of all bonds to face the Supreme Soul".[10] Thus freed, we can live fruitfully and intensely, without fearing the conquering enemy—death.

These four stages of life implicitly point to the twofold perfection woven into our pursuit: "the perfection in being and the perfection in doing."[11] Our employment, or work may produce welcome results, but the inner work—the perfection of one's personality and the inner self supersedes it in immense value and power for good. And how do we define 'goodness'? Tagore says goodness represents the separateness of our spirit from the snobbishness of our egoism. We have to be true to our inner dimension not only for the sake of worldly duties but for spiritual fulfillment.

The Quest for fullness of life necessitates that I face the inevitability of death. Authentically facing death discloses to me the most obvious mark of my finitude. To recognize myself as a being-toward-death nudges me toward a kind of eschatological existence . . . an existence which is oriented toward the ultimate end, while recognizing an urgency and responsibility in living

Intense Life in the Spirit

Both Fromm and Tagore exemplify the need for an intense life of the spirit in personal growth and unfolding. Fromm's requirements for artful living emphasize the need people of the west have for a more interior approach in the Quest for selfhood. Tagore's presentation exemplifies ideally the thinking of eastern folk in seeing the intense life of the spirit in personal growth and unfolding.

Innate in the heart of every individual is the desire for the Supreme Good—the Holy. In the Hebrew world, the Spirit was always invited to inhabit each earthly dwelling. Ancients understood that the restless yearning of the heart was characteristic of every individual. The movement of the heart inward is not characteristic of the Eastern cultures only, though it is perhaps more apparent because their traditions are steeped in the rudiments of inwardness. The blind stirrings toward peacefulness and silent unity of spirit are found within the cultural milieu of the West as well. Seemingly these yearnings are more difficult to extract because of personal and cultural sediments and pursuits. Western affluence, its rapidly expanding technology and economic preoccupations, are great distractions. On the other hand the vast reaches of poverty, hunger and disease vitiate against the longed-for inwardness of millions in the Third World.

The unreasonable pursuit of power, possession and pleasure runs counter to the whisperings of the Spirit. Our swift moving, weltering environment often succeeds in lethargizing the current of spirituality which meanders in us far below the exterior. Though our careless indifference will stifle our spirit it will not efface it! van Zeller assures us that "the current of spirituality is always there, always on the move below the surface. The current never stops, it is only the recognition of it that falters . . ."[12] Unless the spirit is allowed to emerge, we are caught in a polarized, schizophrenic existence. The gifts we are given through the power of the Holy Spirit are reflective of our dignity. We become Christ-bearers through the various gifts we possess. The Holy Spirit is the Giver.

Discipline

All wise teachers, throughout the ages have emphasized the need for discipline. Jesus was no exception. Did he not say, "Whoever does not carry the cross and follow after me cannot be my disciple"? [(Lk.14:27)] Obviously, 'disciple' and 'discipline' have the same Latin derivative, "discipulus" or "discere" meaning to learn. A disciple sits at the feet of the Master to learn. It is still the case today. We cannot be good disciples without restraint, control, attentive listening and practice. The whole of the lifestyle of a follower of Jesus is included in the call. True Disciples of Christ are aware, even today, that the pursuit of the Kingdom should be one of our highest priorities. We are required to renounce all other interests. It is a radical demand, but not different from what God demanded in the Old Testament. Love God with your whole heart, soul and might. $^{(Cf. Duet. 6:5)}$ This can be interpreted in such a way as to mean all one's affective powers. IF my affections are in any way inordinate, for persons, pleasure, money, food . . . , the Lord is calling me to discipline. The Synoptic writers stress discipline primarily as denial. John's Gospel puts an emphasis on the spiritual aspect of discipline . . . the freedom of the true children of God.

Both Fromm and Tagore emphasize the need of discipline in search of our true self. The movement toward wholeness is a discipline. It is an effort to achieve, at all costs, the best that I can be. Nothing is achieved without cost of some kind. The question is, "Am I willing to pay the price?" On the human level, Americans pay exorbitant amounts of money to 'look good' but the inner "look" is often most neglected.

I think discipline can be epitomized in the Chinese proverb, "Find your roots and take wings." Without discipline, the person in search of selfhood is rootless, dissipated, shiftless, one-sided. Discipline provides the rootedness necessary for integrating body and spirit, the interior and exterior dimensions of every person. Discipline liberates both body and spirit and provides the "wings" necessary to soar beyond the bondedness of daily events and mundane ties. Our lives are then freed from rigid rules and regulations imposed upon us from without: an inner strength of willingness and conviction motivates us.

Concentration, too, requires discipline. If I am truly to concentrate I must empty myself of the fidgety, restless, anxious feelings that often have a vise-like grip upon me. Fromm insists that what I am doing at any given moment requires my full attention. Concentration means to live in the present. As in *vanaprasthya,* we find a balance between being distracted by the 'world' and absolutely out of touch with it. In concentration we are drawn to the center, to focus, to intensify our life around a meaningful core. Centering pivots on the NOW. Living in the past, or yearning for the future impairs the practice of concentration and fragments my existence.

A major fruit of concentration is that it facilitates sensitivity to one's self and others. Self-oriented sensitivity does not mean thinking primarily and exclusively of self. Rather, it means living in a state of relaxed alertness. Awareness of the bodily and emotional dimensions of the self is a fruit of concentration. I can respond well to pleasant and invigorating experiences. Neither do I discount the stressful. I can lovingly acknowledge that I am depressed, irritated, or anxious. I become aware of situations which thrust me into joyful or dismal moods which arise as the interchange between me and my world occurs.

The attitude of patience is the sustaining substratum of the ongoing Quest for selfhood. Lacking patience, I may be prone to give up long before the end of the journey is reached. Silence, reflection and relaxed presence are contingent upon a patient existence. Listening attentively to ones' self may be the most neglected terrain of our Quest. Our very self is the territory that has the stamp and imprint of the Divine. Being in touch with our physical and emotional self is also a way of exploring the deep hidden mystery for which we search. We often find that the body/soul dichotomy still haunts us because the Cartesian split has not been entirely healed. Nevertheless, it is in our earthly-bondedness that we strive for goals beyond the horizons of the world we are exploring.

In the Quest for life, pursuing selfhood is our lifetime task. This pursuit plunges me ever more intensely into life as celebration. From infancy to childhood, young adulthood and mature living, the questions change from time to time to suit the framework of my being. An awareness of life's rhythms sustains me: receiving-giving, loss-gain, hope-discouragement, birth-death . . . an endless list of seemingly diametrically opposed elements. All without exception, however, serve to situate me in an attitude of festivity. The negative characteristics of life accentuate the positive. Shadows emphasize the light. They give beauty and form, depth and color to the emerging whole.

M. GERMAINE HUSTEDDE, PHJC

As I surrender to God's specific design in my Quest for Self-hood, I acquiesce with His grace, to the pattern that is inherent in my givenness. I no longer question unreasonably my limitations, shortcomings, or my specific temperament. I acknowledge my shadow-side with love. All that is part of my make-up is gift. I learn to accept all, as inherent, in the nature I have received. I know that imperfections are part of the ongoing Quest concomitant with taking on "the special form God wants [me] to acquire and which He destined for [me] from all eternity."[13]

NOTES

1. Cf. Raymond T. Bond (ed.), The Man Who Was Chesterton (Garden City, New York Doubleday and Co., 1960) p 119

2. Cf. Johannes Metz, Poverty of Spirit, trans. John Drury (Paramus, N.J.: Newman Press, 1968), p.61.

3. Erich Fromm, Man For Himself (New York: Holt, Rinehart and Winston, Inc., 1947) p.91.

4. Martin Heidegger, Existence and Being (Chicago: Henry Regnery Co.,1965), Cf. p. 11-52.

5. Cf. Adrian van Kaam, Personality Fulfillment in the Spiritual Life, (Wilkes-Barre, PA; Dimension Books, 1996) Pp. 123-153.

6. Ibid, p.134

7. Cf. Luke 10: 38-42

8. Erich Fromm, The Art of Living, (New York: Harper and Row Publishers, 1956), p.107-118.

9. Rabindranath Tagore, The Religion of Man (Boston: Beacon Press, 1961), pp. 198-302.

10. Ibid., p. 202.

11. Ibid.

12. Hubert van Zeller, The Current of Spirituality, (Springfield, IL: Templegate Publishers, 1970) p.24.

13. Cf. Illustrated Concordance of the Bible (GGT, Jerusalem Publ. House Ltd., 1956) Sec. 28.3

Much of the material in this Chapter has been published previously by the author in *Studies in Formative Spirituality—Journal of Ongoing Formation,* Pittsburg: Duquesne University Press, Volume 1, No. 3, Nov. 1980.

IN THE SHADOW OF HIS WINGS

GROWTH . . .

So small was he
The crowd obscured
The One he longed to see.

Burning desire was the fire
That propelled him to the tree
With great alacrity.

VISION!
His yearning now rewarded
The SUBJECT of his quest—
A voice from the crowd
He heard aloud:
"Come down! I must be your guest"

In humble delight
He abandoned the height
Of the sycamore look-out tree.

From the self righteous throng
He heard like a gong,
"Why share this sinner's bread?
Come to our house instead!"

Despised and branded as a thief
Zacchaeus stood his ground!
Face to face with Jesus
He knew what he had found!

And now THE TEST:
What are you willing to invest
To pursue the QUESTION and the QUEST?

FOR REFLECTION:

Zacchaeus was sincere in his Quest. Do I have the same determination?

What is my reaction when 'the throng' stands against me?

How can I be more attentive to the Divine Guest in my life?

CHAPTER FIVE

GROPING THROUGH THE FOG

THE LITTLE KNOWN work of Herman Hesse, SIDDHARTHA[1], is a fascinating story—a pursuit toward wholeness and oneness. It is a story of a searching man in quest for his real self and true wisdom. It is the story of learning to listen to the deeper self and to all reality.

Siddhartha is introduced to us as the son of a Brahmin, beloved and respected by all who knew him. Yet, Siddhartha is "without joy in his heart". He experiences an aching restlessness because his heart is not still. His contemplation and meditation in the shade of the banyan trees, his daily bathing of atonement and the sacrifices in the mango woods do not quell his inner yearnings.

Many questions torment him mentally: Where was Atman? Within his inner Self . . . ? But where was his inner Self? Finding no answer to these questions and being convinced that his father and the holy Brahmin had already taught him all knowledge and wisdom, he would abandon home in search of the Samanas.

With his father's consent and accompanied by his constant companion, Govinda, they set out to join the wandering ascetics, the Samanas. It was Siddhartha's hope that through the ways of fasting and meditation taught by the Samanas, he might so conquer Self as to become empty and thus come to Enlightenment.

Three years pass. Discipline and ascetical practices are not sufficient to enable Siddhartha to attain his goal. So the search continues. This time the searching pair go in pursuit of the Budha, the Illustrious One. Both listen to the holy man, Gotma, with eager expectation. They were duly impressed.

Siddhartha, however, came to the solid conclusion that no-one could find salvation through teachings alone. He also deeply believed that no-one could truly communicate the secret of the experience of Enlightenment–a person would have to experience or discover this within himself. Govinda, on the other hand pledges allegiance to the Budha; so Siddhartha goes his way alone.

Aloneness is a deeply purifying experience for Siddhartha and in it he experiences a kind of awakening. He finally realizes that he is a mystery to himself. He realized that he was in search of himself and that he wished to learn more about his character . . . to rid himself of the Self in order to conquer it. Though these thoughts and goals occupied the mind and heart of Siddhartha, he felt that there was nothing in the world that he knew less about than himself.

Though Siddhartha only gradually comes to the awareness that he is a stranger to himself, he no longer tries to escape himself. He gives himself to listening and learning what the secret of Siddhartha is. In this new approach, the world too, suddenly becomes transformed. Everything took on new meaning and depth. Nature, which before had been a "fleeting and illusive veil before his eyes",[2] and which Siddhartha had regarded with distrust, was perceived with new vision.

Siddhartha continues his journey . . . searching. He comes to the river—a symbolic boundary between two worlds and two modes of life. Crossing the river, Kamala and passionate love, Kamaswami, money and business, dice and riches become his life. Siddhartha is now wise with worldly wisdom and possession but the gentle, still voice within was not silenced. Siddhartha was graced into the awareness that real life was "flowing past him".[3] Now and again, the still voice complained as Siddhartha retreated less and less into his very core, but the persistent voice was hardly more than a whisper.

The Gift of a Dream

Eventually, Siddhartha disgusts himself with the pursuit of pleasure and possession. The affluent sickness of the rich crept into his being and filled his soul. It left him inert and hapless until one night the gift of a dream awakened him to the shallowness of his living. In a kind of retrospective stance, Siddhartha is called to remember times in his life when he felt genuine joy and peace. He is called to face things that are troubling him; the fear of growing old, a life un-fulfilled. Listening to this inner dream voice, Siddhartha once again becomes a searching pilgrim.

Early next morning, Siddhartha abandons his wanton ways and wanders back through the forest to the river he had crossed earlier. Remorse and anguish hang heavy in his heart. In self detestation, disgust and despair he is tempted to commit suicide. But from somewhere deep within, or from the movement of the rushing river, the sound of the sacred OM emerges. Siddhartha uttered aloud the holy OM as he beheld his countenance in the water. With OM resounding in his ears the devastating folly of his intended action breaks upon him.

Sleep overtakes him—healing restorative sleep. When he awakens he finds Govinda, his childhood shadow, watching over him. Siddhartha tries to explain his continuing search—

> *It is the same with me as it is with you my friend.*
> *I am not going anywhere. I am only on the way.*
> *I am making a pilgrimage.*[4]

Again Govinda goes his way alone and Siddhartha reflects deeply on his past. His reflections lead him to new awakenings and a great happiness surges up within him. Siddhartha comes to realize the evils of a worldly life. Now Siddhartha realizes, too, that "no teacher could have brought him salvation."[5]

Now he listens with new ears and the river gazed at him refreshingly. It seemed to him that the river had something special to tell him. Siddhartha wanted to live by the river and learn from it. From the river and Vasudeva, the ferryman, Siddhartha learned a great deal. He learned a new consciousness regarding the unity of life. He learned how to listen . . ."to listen with a still heart, with a waiting, open soul, without passion, without desire, without judgment, without opinions."[6]

M. GERMAINE HUSTEDDE, PHJC

Finding the Way

We could well peruse the entire book. It could tell us so much about ourselves and our pursuit, our Quest for wholeness and the Holy! Actually, the name Siddhartha means "one who has found the way". Siddhartha's quest was for wisdom. Each of us could characterize our search for Self by defining definitively that for which we search and pursuing it . . . *finding our way*. Siddhartha nurtured a readiness to hear the whisper of the OM that emerged from the rushing waters. It was that still inner voice that called to him and through which he understood the folly of his intended action.

The Hindi word 'OM', means the "Divine Word". The Indian artist, Joti Sahi, teacher and lecturer, has a meaningful art piece which portrays the Scriptural passage "And the Word was made flesh and dwelt amongst us, and we have seen his Glory."[7] What fascinates me the most in this artistic portrayal is the fact that with the quarter moon, and the Spirit, (dove) Sahi creates the letters that form the Hindu word, OM.

The twelfth-century theologian and spiritual master, Saint Bonaventure, (c. 1217-1274) says that "of ourselves we are not able to lift ourselves up; we need a power stronger than our own." Reflect upon the moon as representative of the frail human person and the Spirit as the power in our lives to lift us beyond the pettiness of our fallen nature, to help us come to the transformation which God intends for us. We are most ready to meet God when we are really in search of Him, when we are poised like an Elijah waiting for the "I AM WHO AM".[8] God is always with us but the din of distractions, the rush toward recent mundane revelations, and the noises of the nothingness we pursue, make it impossible to hear the still, small voice. On the other hand, in God's presence all that is dissonant, harsh and distasteful melds into sweet harmony and gives a lilt to our faltering steps.

Except for extremely rare incidences, hearing God's voice is not an auditory experience. Nor is it a single dramatic occurrence. Attentiveness to the call of God, the voice of God, is the work of a lifetime. It is a readiness and an openness to receive. Our openness and readiness must be like that of the downy nest ready to receive the new-born bird, or like the freshly shaped pottery with its inviting space. To hear the voice of the Master, we must not only be poised and ready like the faithful Dog on the old Gramophone, but we ought to cultivate a framework of stillness, an aura of silence. An agitated busyness overlaid with myriad objectives which must be accomplished NOW, will certainly not be the right climate to welcome the still, small Voice. The space within needs to be tranquil, peaceful, calm. To become a welcoming presence, we practice the art of a listening heart, "Lebh Shomea". When we become practiced in the art of listening in the depth of our being, there is a force that moves us beyond the perimeters of our present horizon and we experience a vastness unknown to us before.

Scripture abounds with invitations to listen. This is especially true in the Psalms. Ps. 78 is a good example:

> *Attend, my people to my teaching;*
> *Listen to the words of my mouth.*
> *I will open my mouth in story;*
> *Drawing lessons from of old,*
> *We have heard them, we know them;*
> *Our ancestors have recited them to us . . . .*
> *The praiseworthy and mighty deeds of the Lord*
> *And the wonders he has wrought.*[9]

Without a listening heart, these wonders pass us by!

Another Sister and I became fast friends through the many years I was ministering in Germany. We are often wagering about this and that, really mere trifles, but it gets our poetic juices flowing. The loser of a little wager has to present the winner with a poem she has written. Recently, I received a challenging piece entitled, "HORT, DANN WERDET IHR LEBEN" [Listen and You Shall Live]. It has a fascinating twist, though, like all translations, it loses some of its depth.

LISTEN AND YOU SHALL LIVE

Lay
Your ear on the pulse of your soul,
Listen—and know life.
Strain your inward ears
To the rhythm of the tide
Bringing life in.
Ponder Reality!
With the ear of your heart—LIFE. (sms)

This short poem is resonant of Isaiah 55:3 which invites us, "Do but listen! Here are dainties that will ravish your heart." Listening brings us to the rich fare that God wants to give! It shall gift us with life! What would happen in our Quest for the Living God if we laid our ear on the pulse of our soul? We know how it feels to strain our ears in the physical sense. How does it engage me to 'strain my inward ears'?

The Quakers urge us, "Sink down in silence; grow deaf to hear." Ponder in silence! What image does it conjure up for you? I have often encountered children and persons suffering from hearing impairment. Without exception these persons seem to have an innate giftedness or super-sensitivity in their other senses. They 'hear' through gesture, smile and touch, perhaps 'hearing' more than those with perfect or normal physical hearing. It is stillness that opens the door of the ear to the inner voice of all things, trees, animals, sun and stars, mountains and hills . . . but more especially to God, the Creator.

There is another aspect to this seemingly contradictory statement, "grow deaf to hear"! In order to truly *hear,* to listen well—it is necessary to 'grow deaf' to our pre-conceived ideas, our personal agendas, judgmental attitudes, biases and labeling. How often in Scripture are we confronted with the Chief Priests and Pharisees who could not 'hear' the truth of Jesus' message because they carried too much personal baggage!

Tagore exclaims, "I have dipped my heart into **this** silent hour; it has filled me with love."[9] Love is the reward of nurturing stillness. It is a jewel of great price. To facilitate growth in self-knowledge we must become centered, focused on what we are about, plumbing the depths! It is only in stillness that we can hear God's voice. This 'stillness' is that inner quality that pervades even in jubilant song and rejoicing!

Where and how can we find the "silent hour"? It is worth the search because the find is so great and rewarding. Is it important for me to be protective of a small space of time each day, to nurture solitude, to sit as it were, "alone on the roof", to develop a desert space in my busy, undulating world?

The Psalmist urges us, *"Be still and know that I am God."* (Psalm 46) There are two vital elements in this short statement. Both are admonitions which are essential for inwardness—for mysticism. *"Be still* and *know"!* Being still requires surrender and receptivity. We have said previously, but it bears repeating that it is in solitude, in readiness and with an attitude of worship that I am brought to God. *"Know that I am God"!* WE do not come to 'know' God through a process of reasoning. God is mystery and a matter of the heart. The 'knowing' is experienced as a felt union, an intimate experience as a readiness for surrender. A medieval view puts it this way: *A stretching out of the soul into God through the urge of love.*

Sometimes we can come to this 'knowing' through a kind of personal amanesis—remembering. When was the first time I had an awareness of the truth that God loves *ME?* What is my most cherished experience of God in prayer? . . . my most awesome finding of God in nature? in another person? the day I experienced that God really loves me because I felt the weight of sin lifted from me? This sort of reflection requires a listening at the deepest level of my self—at the very center of my being. It is as though I allow myself to be immersed in a sunny, calm, quiet environment of listening. When I remember through the warmth and light of God's grace, my response is one of grateful acceptance and re-affirmation of the truth that God loves ME!

Recall or remembering, hinges on God's manifestation of Himself through some special grace. Remembering can serve as a sort of measuring rod telling me of my attempts to know God.

Followers of the Way

—and so we continue on the WAY. Jesus Himself told us "I am the WAY, the TRUTH and the LIFE.[10] I am sure you remember that the early Christians were often referred to as 'Followers of the WAY'. Jesus is our best Example and our best Teacher. The Way that Jesus marks out for us is that of adhering to the will of the Father. In other words, complete surrender! Our quest for the search of our inner self can meander along many paths, but there is only one WAY that leads to the depth of the true self. Sincerely following the WAY requires a deep personal relationship with Jesus—a guarded, inner relationship along with a renewed daily commitment! Dag Hammarskjold commented in his journal, MARKINGS, that "the longest journey is the journey inward." It takes a long and persistent effort to come to the depths. C.S. Lewis expressed graphically the awareness that God dwells in the deepest recesses of our heart and it is from that vantage point that God's call surges up within us . . . but it is not our doing! As C.S. Lewis remarks "Only God can let down the bucket into the depth of us".

God's call often harbors an element of surprise. Perhaps we recognize it symbolically if we recognize it at all. For Siddhartha, the river which seemed to smile at him, which reflected his face and which uttered the still small word OM, was the symbol which he needed most at that particular moment.

Can you imagine that Siddhartha told his story many times to his friends and reminisced about it with Vasudeva? Our life too, is a story—a narrative that links various sequences together. Objectively, it is the pulling together of many events and happenings. But the more precious aspect is that subjectively, the story has to have an identity—it is MY story, MY search, MY journey.

My Story

In our story, there will be two urges manifested: the one is toward selfhood, individuation and separation; the other toward an escape from the loneliness of self into something bigger than the self. These two urges are constantly in tension with one another. We cling to self-hood [self-love] reluctant to let go, yet at the same time we have an inherent longing for union with something (Someone) beyond ourselves. This is the whole plot around which the story of SIDDHARTHA is built.

Often we cannot hear the call of God until we come to what one of my Professors dubbed "ego-desperation". Unless we "own" the isolation, insecurity, loneliness and dread, experienced by all the mystics, we live too much in our ego-world. On the other hand we must realize that the desire for union is far stronger on the part of God than it is in ourselves. Scripture confirms this a thousand times over. God searches for us! God is ever stooping down to us in our humanness and need. It is in reciprocity that we experience joy and in which the call of God becomes apparent. It is the thread that is woven into the book of Exodus and throughout Scripture.

Our Exodus story, as well as that of the Israelites calls us again and again to say "yes" to the God who wants to free us . . . to bring us to new level of wholeness and peace. But like the Israelites we are slow to say an unreserved 'Yes'. We balk at the things that are good for us. In Exodus, we read of God speaking to Moses and telling him that he has witnessed the conditions and suffering of His people. Yahweh then told Moses that he would come down and rescue them.[11] Our Exodus requires that we acknowledge our need, but also that we trust that our God is just as desirous to befriend us as He was to deliver the Chosen People of Old. Moses had encountered the Living God at the manifestation in the Burning Bush. He approached this startling phenomenon with openness and alacrity and a large amount of inquisitiveness. In our journeying it would be easy enough to miss the new and challenging presence of God perhaps because we concentrate on the wrong things. Maybe we are too fixated on the road itself, the rocks, the dust or the potholes, or even our own personal 'brokenness'. We are not always responsible for the latter, but we are responsible for our mending!

Even as God lays out the plan and telling Moses the part he is to play in it, Moses is formulating objections and excuses in his own mind: " . . . I don't know what to call you. . . . they won't listen to me! . . . I am not a good speaker!" Does it remind you of some of the ways we respond to the call of the Spirit in our lives?

Our living-dying-rising is an exodus event which we continue to celebrate throughout our life's journey. We have to learn to live, as did the chosen People, to trust the loving God who started us on the way by calling us into being. Perhaps we can look backward some thirty, forty or more years and recall how the Providence of God has sheltered, guided us and nourished us along the way. Just as it took the Chosen people a long time—forty years of wandering in the desert—to come to complete surrender . . . so, too, does it take us a life-time to be formed as His beloved. The secret lies in the assurance of God Himself who promised, "I am always with you! It is God's doing, more than our own, that sustains us on the journey. It behooves us to learn to rest in Him. There we gain the strength, the insight and the wisdom to follow the right path. He is the life-giving manna and the water from the rock!

In the play entitled "SANYASI" [Acscetic]—also written by the Indian poet Tagore, a traveler [searcher] asks the Sanyasi, "Can I get shelter in this place?" The Sanyasi replies: "Shelter, there is nowhere, my son, but in the depth of one's self. Seek that; hold it fast if you would be saved." It is in the depths of self that we encounter Him who called us into being, journeys with us and who longs to celebrate life with us now, and for all eternity.

NOTES:

1. Herman Hesse, Sddhartha, trans. Hilda Rosner, (New York: Bantam Books, 1991),
2. Hesse, Op. Cit., p.45.
3. Ibid., p.71.
4. Ibid., p. 95
5. Ibid., p.99.
6. Ibid., p. 106
7. Jn. 1:14
8. I Kings, 19: 12
9. Rabindranath Tagore, Collected Poems and Plays of Rabindranath Tagore, (London: Macmillan London Limited, 1977) CLXX P. 309
10. Jn. 14:6
11. Cf. Exodus 3, 6 ff.

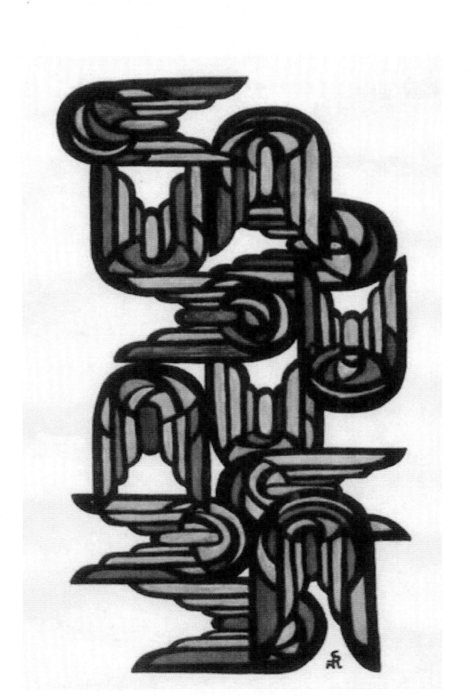

MEDITATION

WHY

O mystery God,
Vast planet space
Is your secret hiding place.

Eternal One, super-wise
You've chosen simple earth disguise-
Burning bush and fireflies.

O loving God,
Vast planet space
Is your abiding dwelling place.

Emmanuel, God enfleshed—
Sent to be an earthen Guest,
Invitation and the Quest.

O hidden loving mystery, manifest theophany
Why do you hide where you abide?

FOR REFELECTION:

Do you feel, sometimes, that God is hiding from you?

Where have your experienced God's disguise?

Have you experienced God as Invitation, Guest or Quest?

What did you learn?

CHAPTER SIX

WHAT'S IN A NAME?

HAVE YOU EVER wondered, reflected or meditated on the passage "To everyone who conquers, I will give some of the hidden manna and I will give a white stone, and on the white stone is written a new name, that no one knows except the one who receives it."[1]

This passage speaks to me about the intimacy God wants to share with each one of us. What is the hidden manna? What is the white stone? . . . and the new name? These precious words can be experienced as God's call inviting each of us to search for the hidden meaning. Of the three subjects—hidden manna, white stone, and new name, the latter intrigues me the most.

With a new name comes a new identity. Recall Abram to Abraham, Sarai to Sarah, Jacob to Israel, Simon to Peter and Saul to Paul. Names in the East were not merely social labels conveniently employed to distinguish one person from another or one family from another. For the Semite the name always expressed something of the inner nature of the person. The name change effected by God in the case of Abraham and Sarah signified the special possession which God took over their lives. Is the whole of life our quest or journey to attain that new name, written on a white stone which the bearer alone will know?

God Journeys With Us

Scripture delineates God's journey with His people. From creation through the loving Contract or Covenant, through the oft-repeated forgiveness of errant human kind, to the dispatching of His own Beloved Son to save us—God is faithful. Through His gracious mercy, Salvation and Victory are at hand. *Who wins the victory; who conquers?* It certainly is not our singlehanded conquest! It is through our repeated returning to God, repenting of our waywardness, walking with Him in good and difficult times, and thus discovering through His light, our true identity. I perceive that the white stone is symbolic of the victorious one and that the new name is being fashioned from the "stuff" of our living. It is important to look at how I am journeying through life.

Do I find that I am wont to weave myself into a tight cocoon of security, self-will? Unlike for the butterfly, this 'darkness' leads to stagnation and death. In this state we can feel nothing but self-imposed isolation and alienation. We are living in a cramped, limited space that is not at all life-giving.

How do we become a beneficiary of the wonderful gift of life God has given us? In a sense that is the wrong question because all through life, we are its beneficiaries! In its deepest and most original sense, our heritage hinges upon our _Dasein,_ our 'power to be' which was the gift God bestowed upon me at the first moment of conception. Birth ushers me into the mode of 'becoming'. As I grow and mature, I choose to be in a certain mode of searching, for example, and I cannot at the same time, be _not_ searching. When I lock myself into a prison of self-will, I cannot simultaneously, be free.

But our journey through life is always developing on two planes, the physical and the spiritual. In both instances the wayfarer needs food. In our society of "plenty" we are not apt to miss the three 'squares' a day. It is not a given is a society that scrimps day after day to find sufficient food for existence.

On the spiritual level nourishment is also a requirement. Daily, we are gifted with the "hidden manna" though we seldom attend to it. Does it come in the form of daily nourishment we receive from Scripture? Jesus is the WORD made flesh, Who dwells among us. Even in the natural order, one of the main properties of the WORD is its availability. Different from most other created things, a word is diffusive. Once it is spoken, it is available to all who are within earshot. I cannot claim it any more than you! A word is equally, totally and simultaneously present to all who have heard, depending of course, on the disposition of the hearer. A word becomes ours only in so far as we take it to ourselves, believe in it and allow it to take root in us. We recreate it, as it were, and bring it to birth. The difference lies in the heart of the receiver. We take the word of Scripture, for instance and ask God to give it the breath of the Spirit so that it springs to life in me. It is the same with JESUS, THE WORD! If the presence of Jesus which I possess through the gift of Baptism is to come to full flower in me, I must cultivate a welcoming, listening, responsive presence to the WORD. The essence of Christian Sannyasi, (placing or depositing my whole being into God) lies in our participation in the WORD-BOUND life of Jesus. This, begun in His Incarnation, moves through dying on the Cross, to Resurrection. The WORD of God will have little effect in our lives unless we learn to be truly hospitable to it. We must welcome the Word and allow it to resonate within us, to linger with it as with a treasured guest such that it makes its home within us.

In prayer, I take the event, for example, the Storm on the Lake, and visit it as though I were in that same boat. (Cf. Mk. 4, 35-40) Do I perhaps feel that Jesus has lost interest, care or concern for me? Do I hear the question which Jesus posits, "Why are you fearful?" Do I allow myself to *hear* the question and to make the Gospel passage my own? Can I sit hospitably with the WORD and be assured again that I am loved, that Jesus is always with me in my laughing, dancing moments as well as in moments of fear, doubt and distress? The Constitution on Divine Revelation (#21) assures us that it is in the Sacred Books that the Father in heaven meets the children on earth. This meeting results in dialogue, the Father speaking with the children, and it becomes food for the soul.

Is it in the encounter with Christ in Eucharist that I find nourishment and refreshment? The Eucharist is a special encounter with Christ and the most profound spiritual nourishment. The Eucharist calls us to thanksgiving. It is the re-enactment of the total sacrifice of the Beloved Son of the Father. Through Him we have remission of all our sins, faults and shortcomings. Only in Him are we made whole. At the consecration of the Holy Mass, after I adore the Sacred Species, I have, for years, prayed a small prayer in my heart—I know not if it be of my own making or borrowed, but it has become *my own:* "Gracious God, cleanse me of all my iniquities;

make me whole and sustain me in Your love." It is manna for me and then when, a few minutes later, I receive the Eucharist, the Body and Blood of Christ, I feel certain that my little prayer has been ratified.

Do we find hidden manna in contact with family or by the visit of a dear friend? The trials, joys and sorrows of friends can be trysting places where we find nourishment and healing for our own lives. Is there real nourishment for me in times of silence, aloneness and prayer? The saints, in their journeying, show us the necessity of a genuine nearness to our God. St. Francis de Sales has left us with the unadorned truth: "Stay close to God! The gentleness of His shadow is more healthy than the brightness of the sun." Like the Psalmist, we can say "I will take refuge in the shelter of your wings"[2].

Nearness to the Source

So how do we stay 'close to God'? The God whom we pursue in our pilgrimage through life is not clearly seen. Our God is a Hidden God, a God of profound mystery. "No one has ever seen God!"[3] On the other hand, our God is intimately close to us through the indwelling of the Holy Spirit. We are called to give ourselves over to the action of the diffusive love of God and to let it spill over into our dealings to all with whom we meet. The Eucharist invites us to live in God's presence, but this reality can easily escape us as our lives become too laden with cares of the day.

Teresa of Avila, who is renowned for imagery in her writings, makes apt use of the butterfly as an image of the soul itself whose commission it is to pass through the stages, or phases, of life to grow into God. Before we pursue what meaning Teresa gives to the butterfly, consider what the butterfly symbolizes for you. I had a friend who was very much into Monarchs. It was her delight to spot the milk-weed plants that attracted the butterflies to lay their eggs. Then came the counting of the worms, the chrysalis, and finally the birthing of the butterfly itself. She joined teams in the tagging of the butterfly, such that its migratory patterns could be charted and monitored. Laura was so into butterflies that she wanted that symbol on her tombstone. Their life pattern and cycle meant a lot to her and she learned many of life's secrets from the creature itself. With the butterfly she journeyed into new and eternal life. She often spoke of the butterfly's vibrant coloration. The colors symbolized virtues and attitudes for her. "Look at that golden orange", she would say. "Doesn't that speak of gratitude?"

Letting nature speak to us is another means of drawing nearer to our God. When we pray Scripture, it becomes obvious to us that Jesus himself loved nature and used it to effect many of the miracles He worked. Can you again hear Jesus saying "consider the lilies of the field" when you feel tired and burdened? The parables abound in things of nature: seed, water, fields of grain. Can we imagine that each element of nature was a source of His praise and closeness to God the Father? Gratitude is a stance of those who live from the inside out! They are people with a heart and their living exemplifies the depth of this mystery.

Some of the elements which the butterfly symbolizes for me are beauty, sensitivity, and transformation. We cannot live without beauty. We might survive, but can we truly live? There is an ancient Italian adage that says, "If ever you are so poor that you have only two coins in your pocket for bread, use one to buy a flower." The spirit, as well as the body, requires nourishment. Awareness and appreciation of beauty is somewhat of an index as to the degree one is growing into full human stature.

Sometimes beauty takes the form of orderliness, a sense of security and being rewarded with the human dignity one deserves, treated lovingly and respectfully. I recently heard the witness of two young women who grew up in deprivation, chaos, clutter and abuse. Both spoke of an indescribable hunger and longing, not only for food, but more so for understanding and appreciation. They longed to be set free of the bondage of being treated as "things"—useable, disposable, 'throw-away' objects. Overwhelmed with feelings of loneliness, and depression, one confessed to being suicidal during her early teens. The saving grace which came to each was in the form of a "Shelter" that provided the environment each was looking for. Now they were respected, given an opportunity for education, food was provided but most of all there was love, order and a "beautiful" home. The Shelter is extremely simple with only the absolute necessities, but it has an abundance of love and that is what makes it 'beautiful'.

A person who can experience awe at the magnificence of a glowing sunset, or a lovely rose is a person pulsating with life. Such a person is truly contemplative, for to gaze at beauty and be nourished and enlivened by it is to nourish the spirit. To listen to lovely, lyrical music . . . to be awed at the cascading waters of Niagara, or the magnificence of the Grand Canyon . . . to feast one's eyes on the splendor of a starry night, is to drink in beauty. To assimilate beauty, to drink it in, is food for the mystic. Yet all beauty is finite but the things of beauty draw us to God and can bring us to an overwhelming sense of God's awesome presence. Our God is not distant, far-away, unreachable! Did He not say many times over in Scripture, "I am with you"? God needs to become a real presence for us, a loving presence. It is through immersion into the Infinite that we are gradually caught up into endless and limitless Beauty. The Psalmist tells us that the "one thing" we ought to seek is "to gaze on the loveliness of the Lord all the days of our life."[4]

The sensitivity of the butterfly is hard to miss. It blithely, gently alights on the flower sensitive to the brilliance of color and fragrance. The butterfly dwells in silence. It makes no sound. In quiet awareness it goes its way, achieving the purpose for which it was created. Observe the butterfly. It is selective. It does not light on every flower, but chooses from among the array. Selectivity is part of sensitivity. Like the butterfly, we must rest a bit, savor and enjoy what has been found and make life-giving choices.

Sensitivity is often lacking in our overly active, business oriented world. We are too matter of fact, too task-oriented to bother about feelings, too quick to move from one thing to another. Sensitivity is a matter of the heart and also of discipline. Consider the need for making choices. Day in and out we are faced with choosing from among myriad options. When I am not sensitive to my authentic needs, to what is good and appropriate for me and allow myself to be sabotaged by my wants, the choices I make do not lead to growth-producing fulfillment or satiety. Rather they are like flimsy wisps that fade away in the sun, leaving me gorged with nothingness.

Transformation is an essential quality in the life-cycle of the butterfly. The worm that spins the cocoon is fat and unsightly. However, in the deep, still darkness, in the waiting, the new life is born. Consider the fact that the worm gives its entire self so that the butterfly can emerge. Truly, in this dying to self, beauty is brought forth! The transformation is so complete that one can no longer recognize its origin. The transformation that takes place from the unsightly worm to the beautiful butterfly effects the realization of its deepest originality. This realization is the goal too, of my entire life's journey.

For many centuries the butterfly has been depicted in Christian art as a symbol of the Resurrection. It is a sign of our share in the victory of Christ over death. As a very unattractive earth-bound worm, this small creature enters its cocoon for a death-like sleep. When the time is right, it bursts forth from its captivity into new life. Timing, patience, gradualness and complete surrender are all apropos for our transformation as well.

For Teresa[5], the butterfly analogy is even more replete with meaning. She says that the worm is like the soul which takes life through the energy which comes from the Holy Spirit. Using every help that comes from God it comes to full growth and begins to spin the cocoon in which it is to die. The cocoon, for Teresa is comparable to the fifth mansion where we become oblivious to all externals. Our minds and hearts are caught up into the things of God. She turns 'architect' telling us how to build the cocoon. We are to renounce self-will and self love, and our attachment to earthly things. We need to practice penance, mortification and obedience, and finally, be absorbed in prayer. When the cocoon appears "dead to the world"—only then the new life emerges as a white butterfly. She says, "Let the silkworm die—let it die as in fact it does when it has completed the work it was created to do. Then we shall see God and ourselves be completely hidden in his greatness as is this little worm in its cocoon"

Teresa goes on to tell us that a butterfly is born restless. She says that it does not know where to make its abode. By comparison with the quiet and security of the cocoon—everything leaves it dissatisfied. It cannot be satisfied any longer, for it has wings now and it must fly! Teresa says now the butterfly feels a stranger to things of earth and it forever goes about seeking a new resting place. As Pilgrims, Wayfarers, we are also motivated to seek the place of our rest. This can only happen when we are in full communion with our God.

Our transformation is of God. We hold our treasure in earthen vessels. It is the power of God at work in us that effects our ultimate change. My mundane, ordinary, everyday self is exposed to the transforming power of God. The re-creative warmth, the sun of His love and the power of the Holy Spirit bring me to new life in Christ.

The Spirituality of Awakening

Listening is the spirituality of awakening. As we are awakened to life, we recognize the activity of the Spirit. "It is the Spirit sent into our hearts in Whom we cry out Abba—Father."[6] We certainly must depend on the Spirit because here we are not talking about the ordinary, but rather about reflective listening—listening with the heart.

Lao-tze, the Chinese philosopher says, "The greatest revelation is in stillness." Julian of Norwich has some advice for us as well: 'Do not disregard the importance of stillness in learning to listen' and Meister Eckhart reminds us that God speaks his word ONLY to the truly tranquil soul. Of Kierkegaard, the famous Dutch philosopher, it is said that as his prayer became more and more recollected he himself had less and less to say. In his tranquility, he became more than just a non-talker, he became a listener. It behooves us to become reflective. Only then the soft spoken inner voice can be heard. The tumult and noise of perpetual motion overpowers the still small voice and crowds it out of our daily living. Without a deep inner posture authentic attention to the Divine is impossible. Without it, our lives are purposeless and insipid. Our movement toward the Eternal is what makes human life different from that of bird, beast, flower or butterfly. It is only in stillness and listening, with the heart, that I become aware of the spirit dimension of myself.

We cannot come to full maturity without moments of silence and solitude. Indeed, longer intervals of seclusion and retreat need to be set apart in order to reflect, to drink deeply of the mystery of life and to be renewed. After long hours of preaching, miracles and journeys, Jesus Himself felt the need to go apart, to rest, to pray, to enjoy communing with His Father. He spent the whole night in prayer!

There is really something special and different about prayer in the still of the night. All traffic has ceased, the hub-bub and clang of the day is stilled. Even the birds are silent. Allowing the aura of stillness to envelop one, makes for a unique prayer environment.

I have found that the Quakers have a keen sense of the need for silence. Many of their writings convey this awareness. Dorothy Gilbert Thorne informs us that "at the very center of Quakerism, there is a place of utter quietness where spirit with spirit can meet"[7] It is in this encounter that all the busyness of everyday falls away and we encounter the inner light and peaceful benediction.

A meeting of my spirit with the Divine Indwelling Spirit is prayer at its best. The moments of prayer may pass in silence, but we come to dwell in the Inner Light and experience the special benediction that such prayer imparts. Prayer opens our heart to God and makes the speech of the soul audible to Him.

A little reflective poem that I have written tries to capture this rhythm and relish Love's benediction.

GOD'S NURTURING

Under the shadow of God's wing
I'm safe; sure of protection.
Even in stress my spirit sings—
Contented with abjection.
I relish the peace God's goodness brings,
It is my due conviction,
Thus sheltered in God's nurturing
I am wrapped in Love's benediction.

Quiet reflectiveness and recollection, help to put my journeying, my emerging, my life, into the proper perspective. The tendency toward reflection is not something that we acquire. It is given to us. Our sophistication and functionalized mode of life has taken its toll on the quality of our stillness and peacefulness. We have to be where the action is! This concentration on activity generates restlessness, frustration and fragmentation. In this mode of being, I merely go through the motions of living. I never really take time to relish life.

People today find it very hard to be still. Radios and televisions play everywhere—in the home, the bank, the supermarket, the dentist office ... On the go, headsets accompany us and bodies move in rhythm with whichever beat happens to fill the air waves. Quiet recreations at home with family are almost unheard of. Our lives have become more complex, active, and restless. As an ancient European philosopher, Angelus Silesius, has said, there is nothing that does not move us: 'You yourself are the wheel which turns and turns and finds no rest.'

Finding the Balance

The challenge all through life, however, is finding the right balance between the vertical and horizontal dimensions of my living. I cannot neglect activity, responsibility and apostolate in search of "sweet contemplation". The many areas of social concern demanding responses cannot be ignored by a person determined to progress in a way of "spirituality". The result of such over-emphasis on the vertical dimension might lead to some sort of fanaticism which would express itself in a kind of pseudo-piety.

Too much emphasis along either the horizontal or vertical planes will tend to effect disfigurement. A proper blending of the two will strengthen the fabric of life and produce a consonance or harmony in daily living.

Nothing of what comprises my life leaves me unaffected. Simultaneously all that I do and *am,* influences each facet of my life and those with whom I come in contact. In this daily lived interaction of myself and my 'world' I may come to authentic self-actualization and personal development. And that brings us full circle. Spiritual development cannot take place in a disembodied sprit. However, I am free and able to make choices. Yet even so, freedom is not absolute. It is governed by facticity, (that which I already am) as a human being. Facticity and potentiality are interrelated in the person I am and therefore I can strive toward that which I have not yet achieved. Clearly, on the physical level, I have limitations but in the

M. GERMAINE HUSTEDDE, PHJC

realms of the spiritual I am as free as Jonathan Livingston Seagull to scale the heights. When I give all my limitations and potential into the hands of God, the Holy Spirit carries me along and I can move more freely and lovingly along the path of life.

NOTES

1. Rev. 2:17
2. Psalm 61:5
3. Jn. 1:18
4. Ps. 27:4
5. E. Allison Peers (Ed. & Translator) <u>Interior Castle</u> (Image Books Ed. NY, 1961) p.105-106
6. Gal. 4:6
7. Dorothy Gilbert Thorne <u>Poetry Among Friends</u> (Lebanon, PA: Sowers Printing Company, July, 1963) pg. 31.

RADIANT FLOWERS/WISDOM'S GARDEN

SOPHIA

Sophia, Wisdom—benevolent, bright,
Outshining constellations of the night,
Reflection of God, be my light!

Sophia, Wisdom—subtle, sure,
Healing faults, effecting cure,
Mirror of God's love, be my allure.

Sophia, Wisdom,—radiant flower,
untarnished Spirit of God's power,
Image of Goodness, be my dower.

Sophia, Wisdom—beauty enthroned,
More costly than a precious stone,
Mystery of God, lead me home.

FOR REFLECTION:

What special aspect of Wisdom do I personally need for MY interior journey?

What healing effects have I experienced through Wisdom's instrumentality?

What gift shall I pray for to enable me to meet God in silent ingathering?

M. GERMAINE HUSTEDDE, PHJC

CHAPTER SEVEN

THE MEASURE OF RIGHT LIVING

EVEN GOD WAS impressed by the gift which King Solomon asked for himself. You recall that in a dream God said to Solomon, "Ask what you would like me to give you." Then Solomon spoke to the Lord about the situation in which he found himself. He became King at a very early age of myriads of peoples, and was unskilled in leadership. He replied to the Lord then, "Give your servant an understanding heart to judge your people and to discern right from wrong . . ." Solomon begged God for true wisdom, and discerning judgment to guide the people righteously.[1]

In the realm of the spiritual, we can say with Solomon, "I am very young and unskilled in leadership", even if we have moved far into the span of our years. In the spiritual dimension, we are always beginners. We are always in need of Wisdom to guide us along the right path. We need a discerning heart to know how to choose what is best and sometimes even make choices between good and evil. This is the task of meeting the claims of the spirit in full.

The Many, the Self and the ONE

Side by side with whatever challenges and impediments we meet along life's highway, we have the gift of human consciousness, which we trust is overlaid with true wisdom and graced with the Spirit. This consciousness is always employed at three levels of our existence. In the objective order, we are oriented toward the world. Subjectively, we are bound up with our own person—the Self in all its dimensions. The third dimension, which we will attempt to further focus upon now, is that of the Transcendent.

We could say with Patka, therefore that our consciousness, or "reflection embraces the many, the self, and the ONE"[2] Essentially, these three stages include our unrelenting desire for happiness and for a meaningful life. All through our journey we carry the finite dimension of ourselves. It is the source of our joys, happiness, contentment, etc. limited though they be. Simultaneously, underlying the positive strata of our existence is the bedrock of our imperfections. Our finiteness is like the Pandora's Box housing the tensions, uneasiness, aloneness, failure, as well as the immanent reality of death. We are very well aware of our inability to change this status, though we often live with it in forgetfulness.

Eventually there comes, so to speak, a fork in the road. I may desperately strive to supply for my own deficiencies, or I may opt for the alternative of true wisdom which consists in a make-over of my understanding.

Patka says this consists in coming to a right and in-depth understanding that we can achieve our perfection only by uniting our humanness with the unlimited, infinite perfection of the Absolute.[3]

Opting for this alternative consists in a radical conversion, a turning toward the Sacred. This "turning toward" is not a brief, momentary, single incident that is quickly over and done with. The Sacred, rather, so penetrates our lives that it becomes a value around which all else pivots.

When we become conscious of the Sacred in our lives, we respond with what Otto calls "creature feeling"[4]—a profound mental reaction. This echoes our creature consciousness and hints at that for which we are really striving, namely, losing the self in the Sacred. This *diminishment* is very different from feelings of weakness or dependence. It is a feeling which spills over from the soul like a reflex action. It is more like the cry of John the Baptist who asserted, "He must increase; I must decrease," and "I am unworthy to untie his shoe."[5] The counter movement to "self-depreciation" is to break into praise at the wonders and constant fidelity of the Holy One. Thus the Psalmist in Ps. 145 cries out, "My soul, give praise to the Lord"!

Otto also tells us that this new consciousness brings us to the realization of a special need for atonement. (If we 'toy' with the word, a bit, it becomes at-one-ment!) Atonement is in the service of unification; being caught up in the mystery! Purification! The feelings of awe and fascination bring with

M. GERMAINE HUSTEDDE, PHJC

it a sense of our own unworthiness. "No one is just in God's sight!"[6] Dame Julian of Norwich puts all of this in perspective saying

If we did not fall, we would not know
how feeble and wretched we were of ourselves,
nor would we know so fully the marvelous
Love of our Maker."[7]

Approaching God-consciousness

How do we come to deep, more intense experience of the Holy Other? Our scientific mind and dependency on "How to" modalities would ask for six easy steps. Not at all like wizardry or séance, the means to come to God-consciousness are quite natural. Otto suggests the possibility of art and music to call forth the impression of the Holy, and furthermore, consciousness of a "Wholly Other" is not captivated in words. The saints and mystics resorted to symbols and symbolic phrases in their attempt to convey their meaning.

When Julian of Norwich, for example, experienced how no one can rest until we behold ourselves as nothing compared to God who wraps us tenderly in his love, she was given the image of an acorn. In it she saw the three properties: that God made it, He loves it and keeps it in existence—Maker, Lover and Keeper. Julian concludes: "I may never have complete rest or bliss, that is, until I am so fastened to Him that there is absolutely no created thing between my God and me."[8]

Because we are understanding, meaning-giving individuals, very little stimulus is required to awaken us to an openness to the Holy. It is more like an on-going theme in my life. Daily, I ought to prime myself to await the Lord's coming. How, where, in whom will I encounter the Holy One today? It is this sincere anticipation that readies me to meet the Lord.

I once viewed an hour telecast entitled "Trial by Wilderness". The setting was the Zululand of South Africa. Along with a native guide and wild life expert, five city-oriented young adults braved the wilderness to learn about the dangers and delights of living in the wild. Daily the small band received instructions as to the purpose of the day's journey. Interesting directives were also given as to how the day's instructions were to be carried out. "We will walk single-file—for the most part in silence" was a usual imperative. Hints for safety were given the young explorers, too.

Wide stretches of rolling veldt beckoned the small party. The bush, the vast stretches of the sky, the thinly forested wide-open country—all created an awesome atmosphere. Now and then the group would encounter a fierce looking rhino, a gangly giraffe or a timid zebra. A unique harmony prevailed; the landscape and wildlife complimented one another. The animals seemed to sense that the group meant them no harm.

Very near the end of the expedition when the neophytes had learned some basic information about safety and the ways of the wild, the leader sent each of the young adults off with the instructions that they were to spend three hours alone, in silence, thinking of, and communing with their surroundings.

Through a kind of fast forwarding, the documentary picked up after the three hours and the young adults had wended their way back to the camp. They sat thoughtful and reflective of posture. The leader questioned each of them about their experience of being alone for three hours in the vastness of the African wilds. Hesitatingly, each of the young people expressed something of the feeling they had experienced. One young lady, lively and vivacious, confessed an overwhelming sense of the insignificance she felt. Another described it as a profound experience. Insignificant and profound! Both words seem to relate to something beyond. As I listened to the description of the young folk as they sat around the campfire in the African desert, I was reminded of the directive in the very beginning of Alan Patton's <u>Cry, the Beloved Country</u>: "*Stand unshod upon it for the ground is holy being even as it came from the Creator.*" 9

The words used by these young people to define their experience seemed to connote deeper and more marked meaning than we are wont to give them in common parlance. I am sure that the young lady who spoke about a feeling of 'insignificance' did not mean to imply that she felt this a trifling or petty experience. Her whole tone and demeanor more readily portrayed the radical entomology which signifies a loss of identity—an experience of

M. GERMAINE HUSTEDDE, PHJC

being without sign or distinguishing mark—un-named. Names identify us and they are part of our wholeness.

The lad who spoke of his experience as being profound suggested the quality of silence, the aloneness and the vastness of the experience. These five young people, for the moment, at least, saw far above and below the surface of things and came to an "Aha", peak experience. This safari was definitely a change from what these vibrant youth were used to. Away from the hum of traffic, the hammer of industry, and the hollow chatter of radio, TV, cell phones and companions, each opened up to a broader horizon.

These young people became aware of a certain "creature-feeling", an unconscious awareness of the Holy in the very core of their beings. The situation in which they found themselves awakened feeling of littleness, of insignificance, of dependence. They may have come to the beginning of a prolonged, conscious awareness of the Holy in their lives.

The attitude of expectancy and the willingness to be awakened to something new was an asset which each of the young adults brought with them to this expedition. It turned out to be a blessed time for them. The wilderness uncovered a hidden meaningfulness and portrayed new values—values of silence, simplicity and aloneness.

The Beatitude of 'Nothingness'

Each person that ever lives is basically an openness to the Holy. Innately we possess the beatitude of religious consciousness. We are never without the call of the Holy, but we do not always hear. We become insensitive through monotony and routine. Inner sensitivity may be dulled through gross carelessness and neglect. On the other hand, religious consciousness may lie latent and covered over until some catalytic agent activates it.

In each stage of life there are 'no-thingness'[10] experiences which facilitate the possibility of encountering the Holy. I recall one such incident, years ago when I was privileged to work in India for some years. An emergency arose in northern Madhya Pradesh after one of the Sisters sustained a heart attack and had to return to Germany. Because a large building project was afoot and needed careful supervision, I was commissioned to move to the north.

Though I had a valid residential permit and long-term visa, it was impossible to move from one area of the country to another without informing the local police and the Department of Registration in the other district and state. The Bangalore police were very understanding and validated my request to move out of the 'my area of registration' to attend to this emergency. They agreed to send the proper information to the authorities in Madhya Pradesh. Unwittingly, the communication system must had broken down somewhere along the line. Even upon reporting to the local police after my arrival in Dhani, I was being visited frequently and questioned interminably about why, I was in this district. No answer or explanation seemed to satisfy. After about two months, I was visited by a higher official who demanded my passport. I had no choice but to relinquish it. This left me in a very precarious condition of no credentials whatsoever, and made me very vulnerable indeed. Practically speaking, I became a no-body! In ensuing days as we tried to determine the best mode of action, I often resorted to an adoration time before the Blessed Sacrament. In one such 'visit' when I was particularly distraught, I had a very real sense of the Lord saying to me, "Don't fear! I am always with you."

Shortly, thereafter I made my way to the District of Dhār where the Main Immigration headquarters were located. I retrieved my Passport and all "was well", at least for the time being. To this day, the words "I am always with you" flood into my soul like a balm when the going gets rough. I think I had really encountered a 'NOTHINGNESS' experience which provided the needed break, through which awareness to the Holy was able to seep into my consciousness.

We ask ourselves, what is there in life that can provide this service for us? What can assist us to break out of the shackles of our normal 'taken-for-granted' everyday, safe and secure mode of life? Not everyone is as fortunate as the five young people who were able to spend time in the wilds of Africa or as 'unfortunate' to be stripped of all identity. Even for some, such an experience may not be an opening-up occasion at all.

Actually, one doesn't need such extra-ordinary situations because the very act of living has built in provisions through which one can authentically feel the sensation of "being broken". The adolescent experiences negativity, aimlessness and ambivalent feelings. He feels an urge to criticize. Authority and structure are painful reminders to him of the self that he seeks but which still, so frustratingly, eludes him. This is a kind of negative 'no-thingness' which the adolescent experiences. Through the help of patient adults and significant others, he emerges as a self-presence to the reality around him. Dr. Kraft says that "the adolescent begins to experience a numinous and paradoxical transcendence embedded in a sacred mystery."[11] He begins to experience a new sense of dependency and indebtedness.

Later stages in life have unique and characteristic 'no-thingness' encounters, too. Late adolescence—the late teens and early twenties,—offer possibilities for a positive experience of 'no-thingness'. This is usually a painful time in which the search for identity and the groping toward maturity reach zenith proportions. If left alone, the young person may experience emptiness and the sense of limitation, his nothingness.

The third nothingness experience may invade life in the thirties. By this time, one usually has opted for a particular life-style and is involved energetically in it. Things can run smoothly for a while, but difficulties arise, depression invades one's spirit, loneliness arises and a person is apt to experience failure. Body limits also make themselves felt. A person may even experience the reality of death for the first time. In this nothingness experience, one may be called to re-evaluate, to re-examine commitments and re-dedicate self to take responsibility for what is, and what one wishes to become.

Middle age embodies the crisis of limits. One's limitations increase with age. These limitations become a more potent reality as one draws nearer to one's own death. When one faces the crisis of limits, it may happen that they cloud the vision such that it is difficult to see possibilities because the "perception of a limited present and past frustrate [the] vision of a future."[12]

Old age uncovers yet another aspect of no-thingness. A person's body becomes weaker, physical stamina declines, appetite and sleep habits change. A person may literally feel that he/she is losing one's self. Perhaps bodily control, mental acuteness and ego strongholds all seem to have exited at once.

Sifting and Sorting Life Experiences

These are but a few of nothingness experience we may face on the physical level, but each presents an opportunity to sift and weigh my life in the balance of eternity. Any nothingness experience has the possibility of calling me out of myself to the Holy. It may be that the "negation does away with every 'this' and 'here', in order that the 'Wholly Other' may become actual."[13]

Francois Mauriac's book, <u>The Inner Presence</u>, describes well a nothingness experience. Mauriac himself narrates how well his life had progressed in both the realms of time and eternity. He had been very successful in writing his book, *The Viper's Tangle* as well in the daily ramifications of his life. His health was good, he was successful and everything was 'looking up' until one day in 1932 . . . Suddenly Mauriac lost his voice and was sent to Combloux for treatment. He goes onto tell that this experience in his life was 'like a clap of thunder' and it made a break in his life which created 'a new heaven and a new earth' for him.[14]

As one continues reading the account of this traumatic experience, it becomes clear that this "clap of thunder" became a blessing. The loss of his voice plus the consequent illness did provide a break in Mauriac's smooth-running existence. It is his attitude toward the experience which proves to be the valuable asset. Mauriac makes no secret of his inability to adapt easily to illness. Neither does he hide his effort to transcend the situation saying that even though this was a sickness unto death, he profited from it with the same persistence with which he pursued everything in life. Because of his acceptance and acquiescence in the face of this set-back, Mauriac was able to see a broader horizon. This nothingness experience helped the inner core of his being to emerge.

Not only Mauriac's own life, but the lives of his characters bespeak the spirit dimension of person's lives in their subsequent search for the Holy. Mauriac's novel <u>*The Viper's Tangle*</u>, which was praised so highly, depicts this searching in a miserly old landowner. This embittered and cantankerous old man is on the brink of death but the sputtering flame of life is fanned by love. He responds to that love and dies a changed man.[15]

Nothingness experiences generally lead to inwardness if we allow the spirit-self to dominate. It is impossible to define spirit in a rationalistic way. Attempting to do so would relegate spirit to an object and thus "kill" it. Since the spirit is inward and not of a tangible nature, it is in contradiction to everything within grasp, objective, or conditioned by time or external causes. Spirit cannot be defined by anything that is finite. We therefore resort to note some of the spirit's attributes. Berdyaev lists the following: "freedom, meaning, creativity, integrity, love, value and orientation towards the highest Divine world and union with it."[16] In other words, everything spiritual emanates from the inner depths of our being. As St. Paul reminds us, the body is natural and reaps a bodily reward. But the spirit is the inward, liberating force and always tends toward eternity. It is the spirit that prompts us to rise above the worldly realities, external achievements, power, public opinion and social exigencies.

Getting to the Kernel

In the history of spiritual consciousness, Berdyaev believes that an error has often been perpetrated—that of identifying the soul and the spirit as one and the same entity. We use the words interchangeably without really distinguishing one from the other. He says that the spirit is axiological. It tends toward values such as truth, beauty, purpose and freedom. The soul, on the other hand, is the life principle.

The emphasis once given to Cartesian dualism is shifted by contemporary philosophy and psychology. We are no longer considered an organism compounded of body and soul; rather, *body, soul, and spirit* are considered integral parts of the human personality. Spirituality is not opposed to the body, or to materiality as some would suggest, but "implies its transfiguration".[17] The spirit is the highest quality of the soul, but it may remain undiscovered or suppressed. As Berdyaev remarks, the soul is the kernel of the human creature and the function of the spirit should be to endow the soul with the highest purpose and quality.

Our longing for truth, purpose and beauty is an essential part of our nature. It cannot be relegated to certain moments or phases of life. Abstract interpretation of the spirit results in a false dualism of spirit and flesh, spiritual and intellectual work, on the one hand, as opposed to material and physical labor on the other. Greek intellectualism and Middle Age monastic spirituality unconsciously sustained a body-spirit split. A false and illusory spirituality is born of separation of body and spirit. Such a separation vitiates against human integrity.

Spirituality is part of my *whole* life. The spirit must be the revealing force in every instance of my existence. Whether I work or play or pray, the spirit is the creative attribute. It transcends limitations and stretches toward freedom rather than being bound by determinism. Growing into awareness of my existence as a "self", I realize a deeper identity. I come to know an unchangeable core which permeates and persists despite the changing circumstances in which I find myself. Even though my moods and feelings change the spirit-self behind the 'I' is unchanging.

Too often, we take ourselves for granted. While the inward and outward dimensions of myself are always present, there is a diversity in the emphasis on one or the other. Here the gestalt principle is very much in force. If conscious awareness of my physical self prevails, the spirit dimension of myself recedes and vice versa. The ebb and flow of the inner and outer seem to move in and out like the tide. We recognize that body needs and spirit needs are different, yet the one sustains and supports the other. I'm sure you, too, have experienced that when one becomes occupied and tense, particularly along productive lines, the spirit recedes and the physical dimension comes to the fore. While activity is almost exclusively defined as productivity, accomplishing, and doing . . . the paradoxical situation is that as I work, exercise, paint or play, there is, at the same time, an inner activity which is eclipsed by the concrete goal I have set for myself.

The book I attempt to write, the dough I knead, the floor I scrub . . . productivity of any kind, may push me toward spiritual laziness. I can be active without inner thought or feeling. My senses may be dulled and blurred. An indispensible condition for developing the art of inwardness is that of living on a new level of awareness. The ideal, is to find the element of presence in all that I do. The old adage "Agere quod agis" applies here. "Do what you do!" We can all allow our day to become one puppet performance after another, or I may make an effort to live in an aura of awareness, returning again and again to the reality that God is the Source of my strength, If I rise in the morning, eat hurriedly, go off to work, one day after another, the fetters of habit will become the dominating force. Even my prayer, if I stop to pray, at all, takes on this quality.

We often hear the phrase "division of labor". In the development of my whole self this can become an important practice for me. Certainly, there are demands on the physical plane that need to be met but not at the expense of the development of the whole me. The spirit self is longing for some quiet moments, for scriptural or spiritual reading, for prayer. This is the activity that can become a true labor of love.

If I cajole myself into believing that I can supply the needs of my inner self when I retire or in old age, I am foolish indeed. I need to pause and ask myself, "What am I doing to nurture my spirit? You know that the spirit is the dimension of yourself that is given eternal life. The physical will someday succumb to death; the spirit is destined to live forever. The Scriptural message that we hear so often is invitational and demanding. "Stay awake! You know not the hour when the bridegroom will come! [18]

When I live in such a way that I expect to meet the Bridegroom only at the moment of death, I live in forgetful unpreparedness. The best and most practical way to be prepared is to 'keep oil in our lamps'. I think that in this way we are prepared to meet the Lord even in our everyday, to encounter Him in the most common and unexpected places, in the most ordinary. Such watchfulness will pay dividends when our earthly journey comes to an end, but also on the way of my every day journey.

William Wordsworth, like many poets seems to possess the ability to grow in this inner dimension. In *Lines from Tintern Abbey* the poet extricates himself from the modes of activity and productivity to concentrate on the meaning of life. He enriches life, making a new creation out of the shards of everydayness. The continuum of the poet's existence is such that he tastes the reality of the everyday, transcends it at times and then falls back into the actuality of the everyday world. Wordsworth's beautiful poetic expressions concretize the dimension of the spirit self which longs for the infinite. He has learned that life with all its woes and sadness still has to power to raise one above all the disturbing and distressful situations. He finds something far more precious and 'deeply interfused' that raises a person's spirit and emotions to the One whose 'dwelling is in the light of setting suns'.[19]

There is a bit of the poet in all of us. Sometimes we allow nature to nurture our spirit. We sense something sublime and we transcend the moment, and are drawn out of ourselves to the ONE "whose dwelling is in the light of setting suns." It is the spirit which enables us to recognize, or feel, the Presence of the "something more deeply interfused" similar to Wordsworth's experience. How beneficial to practice the art of wakefulness!

NOTES:

1. I Kings 3: 7-9

2. Frederich Patka, Values and Existence, (New York: Philosophical Library, 1964) P.164

3. Patka, Op. Cit., pp213-214.

4. Rudolph Otto, The Idea of the Holy, trans. John W. Harvey (London: Oxford University Press, 1923) p.51

5. Jn. 3:30

6. Gal. 3:11

7. M.C. del Mastro, Op Cit, p.170

8. Ibid, p 67.

9. Alan Paton, Cry, the Beloved Country, (New York: Charles Scribner's Sons, 1948) p.3.

10. The term 'no-thingness' and the characteristics of the experience as reflected upon here are from Wm. F. Kraft, The Search for the Holy, (Philadelphia: The Westminster Press, 1971) pp. 71-123.

11. Wm. F. Kraft, Op. Cit., p. 87.

12. Ibid. p. 103. The reader may want to visit Adrian van Kaam's work, The Transcendent Self from which Dr. Kraft derived his ideas.

13. Rudolpf Otto, Op Cit., p 70.

14. Cf. Francois Mauriac, The Inner Presence, Recollections of My Spiritual Life, trans. Herma Briffault (New York: The Bobbs-Merrill Co., 1965) p.124.

15. Cf. Francois Mauriac, The Viper's Tangle, trans. Warren B. Wells (New York: Sheed and Ward, 1947)

16. Nicholas Berdyaev, Spirit and Reality, (London: Geoffrey Bles: The Canterbury Press, 1939) p. 33.

17. Nicholas Berdyaev, Op. Cit., P. 39.

18. Cf. Mt.25: 1-13.

19. Cf. William Wordsworth, "Lines from Tintern Abbey" Major British Writers, Enlarged Edition II, (New York: Harcourt, Brace and World, Inc., 1954 p 41.

ROOTEDNESS

AUTUMN CLOWN

Up the hill
On Nister's Mound,
I found Him.

God, the Autumn Clown
Frolicked
The woodland turf
Transforming
Sacred earth.

Receptive,
Barren soil
Embraced each
twirling leaf
Like Love letters
strewn
about my feet.

The landscape of
my heart
Was set aflame,
And where'er I
chanced
to look around,
I found Him-
God, the Autumn
Clown!

FOR REFLECTION:

How would you describe the landscape of your heart at this moment?

When have I experienced the woodland turf transformed?

What name describes your relationship with the Holy Other today?

CHAPTER EIGHT

SOMETHING MORE DEEPLY INTERFUSED

WE ARE FAMILIAR with the story of the Blind Bartimaeus, who sat by the way-side begging.[1] Hearing the turmoil of all the folks tagging along with Jesus, he asked what was happening. When he was told that Jesus of Nazareth was passing by, he called out "Jesus, Son of David, have pity on me." When the towns' folk told him that Jesus was calling him, he threw off his cloak, leapt to his feet and came to Jesus.

If today, miracle or mystery plays were still in vogue as they were in medieval times, one might capitalize on Bartimaeus' throwing off his cloak, leaping to his feet and coming to Jesus! He wanted no encumbrance to get in the way of attaining the gift he sought: sight!

Often it is difficult for us who are sighted to relate to the plight of those with impaired vision, or blindness. I recently experienced this personally as a small blind, orphan boy was brought to our Mission in Kenya. A kindly neighbor accompanied the boy seeking help for clothing, personal items and transport so the boy could be enrolled in the Blind School in Igoji. The good neighbor had assured us that he was not asking for fees; he had already found a sponsor. Little Martin was secure when he heard the familiar voice of the neighbor, but at first he was shy with me. He did not *know* me. Trying to help the boy feel at ease, I pressed a small rubber ball into Martin's hand. He smiled and received the small gift with joy. I told him, "This ball is for you". He looked up and smiled in acknowledgment. We spoke a little more about taking Martin for 'shopping' and purchasing all the items that were on the list that had come from the school. While the Social Worker was being called for this task, I picked up a small plush turtle that was within reach and pressed it into the hands of Martin. At first he recoiled! The feeling was so strange to him. Then I took his fingers and helped him outline the turtle with them. He found the turtle's eye with his index finger and then formed the head of the animal with his finger. Suddenly, the strangeness disappeared and he could "see" the turtle in his hand. It delighted him and he went off joyfully with the Social worker and his friend for the necessary shopping.

But have you also experienced that there are things right before our eyes which we do not see? Several days ago, I was taking care of a little chore that had fallen to me—caring for the plants in the Prayer chapel. Because it was not convenient to water the plants well in the position they were, I put them on a small conveyance and took them out to get a good watering. One of the plants was exceptionally large and beautiful. Along the way, I met a Sister who asked, "Where has that beautiful plant come from?" I was somewhat surprised by the question because it had been in the same place in the chapel for at least three weeks previously. She was as astounded by my answer as I was by the question, when I told her where it had been. Though she passed that way every day, she had not 'seen' it.

Spiritually Blind

Being blind to the visible is rather tragic, but being blind to the invisible is catastrophe. To be aware only of the things we can reach through the senses is to be on the outside of things. Little Martin was on the outside of his new friend, the turtle, until he saw it with his inner eye. His perception of the little creature with his inner senses made it clear to him and he rejoiced in it.

In philosophy class we learned that 'truth is the possession of reality, as it is'. Total reality is only in knowing God as the heart of the world and the world in God. The world of the senses does not, of itself, put us in touch with this deeper dimension.

The blind Bartimaeus must have been keenly aware of his inability to see Christ owing to his physical blindness. All of the visible world escaped him as well, except perhaps that which his senses of touch, taste and hearing provided. Blind people live in a rather isolated world until their other senses take over and "see" for them. So, Bartimaeus, poignantly aware of his plight, raises his voice and shouts as loud as he can, so that Jesus might hear him. He wanted to see! He wanted it with all his heart! We know that Jesus, having asked Bartimaeus what he desired, graciously cured him of his blindness.

Has it ever occurred to you that we often suffer from an inner—a spiritual blindness that we have not even become aware of? This lack of awareness compounds the situation. Because I am unaware, I do not have the necessary motivation or courage, as Bartimaeus did, to call out to God for healing.

Why is it that we can look into the face of another and see only wrinkles time has left, a darkened complexion, a dirty child. We see a person's bodily form but are blind to the goodness, the hunger, the aloneness that another is experiencing. Sometimes we behold a golden sunset, a sparkling stream, a garden replete with beautiful flowers——but we do not see beyond the object at hand. The beauty, seldom or never, speaks to us of the One who created all this loveliness.

The world of creatures has an opaque quality about it. It is as though a covering, blinders, veil the deeper inner beauty. We therefore have a propensity to miss the true meaning of things because its beauty and genuineness are hidden in the heart of God and I just do not see!

Blindness into Sight

Our blindness, lack of vision, constitutes a decisive poverty which I experience as a result of my human condition. It is a poverty that results as deprivation because of humankind's fall from original justice. Throughout my lifetime, I experience the poverty of my unique self. The limitations which bind me are characteristically mine. Lack of vision, unawareness, and shallowness of perception may tend to haunt me. I may methodically attempt to alter this situation in myself. I throw off the cloak of superficiality; I pray for the grace to live in the present, I ask the Holy Spirit to grace me with a new, acute vision. I realize I cannot rely on my own weak efforts. This is key to the spiritual healing of our blindness.

It is a great grace when we have the courage to cry out to God, Jesus or the Holy Spirit as Bartimaeus did. This is the 'first movement' of this great spiritual concerto: 'Blindness into Sight!' But acutely seeing things, in depth, will take practice, concentration and above all love!

In another place in Scripture, Jesus speaks about putting a lamp on a lamp stand so that its light may be seen by all who come in.[2] Jesus goes on to say that "the body has the eye for its lamp; and if the eye is clear, the whole body will be lit up; when it is diseased the whole body will be in darkness."

The forms blindness, or our darkness, can take are manifold. We sometimes let the scales of envy or jealousy blind us to the virtue, generosity or goodness in another. Another person has what we vehemently desire and it blinds us to our own giftedness. Greed may shroud me in darkness, such that I cannot see the misery and need of another. Complacency often blinds me to ways in which I could make a difference in the life of another. I often get caught up in the myopic state of minimalism. Blindness tells me that the least I can do, is sufficient. I cajole myself into the belief that "I really have responded . . . ." and that is all that is necessary.

Saul fell into disfavor with God because he allowed himself to believe that 'what' he accomplished was all that God desired. He responded to God, but not in the way God had ordered him. Saul was to have overcome the Amalekites. God had ordered him "to fight against them until you have exterminated them." He destroyed Amalek but he brought back prisoners and all sorts of plunder and loot to sacrifice to God at a later date. God was displeased with Saul's blind two-facedness and in the end he was dethroned because of it. The Lord does not delight in the burnt offerings. He tells Saul that what God requires is obedience.

Saul is dethroned and Samuel is told by God to look for a new king Obeying God's order, he went to Jesse's house in Bethlehem. Arriving there, he prepared a sacrifice to the Lord and Jesse and his sons were invited. As Jesse presented his sons, one after another, Samuel looked at them expectantly . . . Eliab, was the first and Samuel thought, "Surely, the Lord's anointed is here before me." God cautioned Samuel with the words, "Do not judge from appearance or from his lofty stature, because I have rejected him. Not as man sees does God see, he sees the appearance but the Lord looks into the heart." [3]

We know that of Jesse's sons, David was eventually anointed King. But the relevance of this passage for us here is that authentic seeing is a thing of 'the heart'. God himself gives us the clue. Spiritual blindness cannot be cured without a 'heart surgery' of sorts. I must turn myself over to the Master Physician and allow Him to transform, to cure my inner blindness.

Love is the Cure

Some of the saints spoke of a blindness that resulted from their nearness to Christ. This blindness is much like the experience of returning indoors after having been out in the snow on a sunny day. We are blinded until our eyes adjust to the indoor light. This is a wonderful blindness, but unfortunately, our blindness does not result from too much nearness to Christ or the joy of living in His brightness.

God, in the depth of our souls, is like the brightness of the sun which gives everything a clearer and more perfect view. He lets us see with a new vision. He lets us live in a new warmth—an exhilarating aliveness. It results in a new light step and a grateful heart.

This happens in God's good time. There is a timing in our very lives that is right for growth into the depth of our being. Timing is essential. It was the right time for Bartimaeus to be at the roadside in Jericho just as Jesus of Nazareth was passing by. Perhaps the right time for me is in daily quiet moments of prayerful meditation or recollection . . . perhaps, in the celebration of the Eucharist or some other of the Sacraments. Maybe my eyes are opened as I read Scripture and reflect upon God's infinite love for me. No matter when, there is always an active, responsive willingness required from me. It is the nudge of the Spirit urging me to make room for God. Like Bartimaeus we cast off the cloak and run to Jesus! My cloak may be multi-layered—prejudices, pre-conceived ideas, biases, taken-for-granted modes of existence . . . anything that clutters or gets in the way of my seeing with the heart must be cast off!

Mystics insist that it is the work of God that raises us up, that cures our lameness, our blindness and lethargy. But they are also insistent upon the fact that the Holy Spirit is given us as the vehicle of our transformation. Through the Spirit breathing in us, we enter into God's inner life. It is the Spirit who gives us the wisdom to pray to know those things which are blinding us. We need to pray that we might grow deeper and more intensely in love, for love is the cure!

If we look at Christ in His earthly ministry, we can depict him very readily as a man of love. Jesus infused life into people with the most loving and simplest of means. In the case of Bartimaeus, Jesus stood still and then asked the blind man what he wished for. How extraordinarily simple!

Should not Jesus' action itself show us one of the important ways to come into insightfulness? Jesus stood still! It seems to me that this stillness, quiet pondering, and/or reflective attentiveness is pre-requisite for us to come to the knowledge of what to ask for. Lord, that I may see!"

Help me to see with a clear, unclouded vision where I am evading your goodness, where I am attempting to 'go it alone'! Help me to see the folly of created things while I am forgetful of your Divine Love—the Source of all goodness. Give me sufficient insight to know where I have turned from your love. Fire in me a new awareness of the areas in my life where I have chosen to put my lamp 'under the bushel'. Help me Lord, to reverence my uniqueness and becoming.

St. Paul in his letter to the Ephesians speaks about the necessity to pray for the hidden things in ourselves to grow strong.[4] These are the things which, at the moment, are our blind-spots. He goes on to pray for us saying

> *May you be filled with all the completion God has to give.*
> *He whose power is at work in us is powerful enough to carry out his purpose*
> *beyond all our hopes and dreams . . .*

St. Paul rather hits on a weakness in us. Do we ourselves ask God to bring us to that completeness—the utter fullness of God? Are we fearful to pray so boldly? Do we fail to imagine that God can, and wants, to bring us to wholeness? Do we have dreams that we are fearful to discuss with the

Lord? Bartimaeus was not fearful. He called out loudly, "Son of David, have mercy on me?" Can we not make his prayer our own?

The blind man must have imagined what it would be like once his eyes were opened. This longing urged him to approach Jesus. He must have dreamed again and again of the wonderful gift of sight! Is our failure to ask for our wholeness resultant upon our lack of imagination as to what we truly could become? The power of God is at work in us to carry us beyond all our hopes and dreams—to transfigure us.

Somewhere I have read or heard that true prayer is allowing ourselves to experience "being loved into being." I am sure that as Bartimaeus went on his way that day, with eyes opened wide and a heart filled with gratitude, the lilt in his step proclaimed his sense of 'being loved into being." His was truly a prayer of gratitude. Our blindness so obscures the truth from us that we fail to realize that even at this moment, I am being loved in the same proportion with which God will love me for all eternity.

Following Christ Intensely

The biblical play GODSPELL (somewhat of a medieval mystery drama) contained a very appropriate song prayer for persons intent on new vision:

Oh, dear Lord, three things I pray
To *see* Thee more clearly,
To *love* Thee more dearly,
To *follow* Thee more nearly.

To see, love, follow! This is the pattern for an intense following of Jesus. To journey with Jesus it is imperative that our clouded vision be brought up to 20/20! In the physical world when we go for an eye exam and our vision is found faulty, the optometrist will suggest that the problem be corrected with glasses, or some other form of 'therapy'. In the spiritual domain, the Divine Physician suggests that our faulty vision be cured with a special dose of love. It is only when love is strong enough–when it takes on the dimension of intensity, can we attempt to follow more nearly.

It seems to work in reverse. Following Jesus more nearly, more intently gives me new insights, new awareness and steadfast convictions. Our life with Jesus will result in endless newness and discovery. It will spur a new enthusiasm into each serious person. It will be the renewed presence of Jesus in our life.

When John sent disciples from prison to ask of Jesus if He was the one who was to come or should he look for another, Jesus told those disciples, "Go and tell John what you yourselves have witnessed; the blind see, the lame walk, the lepers are made clean, the deaf hear and the dead are raised to life, the poor have the Gospel preached to them and blessed is the one who does not lose confidence in me."[5]

Jesus response to the disciples of John is an invitation to believe beyond where we are at the present moment. The eyes of faith open up vistas for us that are beyond our imagining. If we allow ourselves to contemplate God's goodness, power and love it is bound to have an effect on our lives and our vision. Once upon a time, I read a pithy statement that went something like this: 'Really contemplating God's goodness is like holding a magnifying glass to the mystery long enough so that God can burn a hole in you'. Igniting this little fire will bring us closer and closer to the ONE who is LIGHT. In Him we will have new sight. This is the "something more deeply interfused"!

We need to learn to walk in that LIGHT. I like the story that Maxie Dunam tells of himself. As a young boy, his father asked him to go to well to get a bucket of water. It was in the days before homes had in-door plumbing and it was already dark. Maxie said he didn't mind getting the water, but he protested because of the darkness. His father, took a lantern off the shelf, lit it, put it in one hand and the water bucket in the other of Maxie. Maxie responded with "But Dad that light is so small" and his father said, "It's all right! Just walk to the edge of the light." Maxie ended the story saying, "Do you know, I never came to the edge!"

If we let Christ be our LIGHT and we walk along with Him, we will never come to the darkness. The Light will always show us the way! More than that, Christ IS the way. His accompaniment never fails because He has secured us in His love as we walk the way with Him.

Notes:

1. Mk. 10, 46-52.
2. Luke 11, 33-36
3. Cf. 1 Samuel 16, 1-13
4. Cf. Eph. 3, 19-20
5. Luke 7, 22-23

AGAINST THE RHYTHM

BLIND MEN

Ten, they were of like demise
Outcasts, all and distanced—
from neighbor, friend and everyone
except in this one instance!

Ten, aware of their awful plight,
stood somewhere off and pleaded:
"Oh Master do take pity!"
and the Gentle One conceded.

Now ten are cleansed, restored, reborn—
set free and mended, whole!
Only a Samaritan returns
grateful, refreshed of soul.

Where are the nine who could not see—
these leper patients, blind?
Border-folk of history
who sought, but did not find!

FOR REFLECTION:

When have I experienced blindness of spirit?

What prevents me from calling out to Jesus for healing?

What ought I to cast off in order to come more freely to my God?

CHAPTER NINE

BECOME WHO YOU ARE

WE HAVE SEEN that overemphasis on the physical dimension of the self tends to orient us totally within the earthly or terrestrial horizon. We want to reflect now on authentic life and peace that is the gift that God wishes to give to each one of us.

The call to life in Christ is the call of every Christian. We uncover ultimate meaning in our lives only through coming to awareness of the Holy and living in, and out of, that awareness. As body-soul-spirit individuals, we find our way toward our deepest and truest self, our originality, against the background of the Sacred.

The life of the Christian is growth into Christ. Fullness of life consists in the attainment of a certain maturity on both the physical and spiritual planes through the day by day process of growth, maturation and self-actualization. Both the physical and the spiritual are gradual growth processes. Just as one cannot measure the extent of physical growth from day to day, neither can we measure the scope or depth of our spiritual growth into Christ, from one day to another, but it is our ardent hope.

We dispose ourselves best, by attempting to embody attitudes that will facilitate personal growth in accord with our unique, basic 'givenness'. Transformation, or growth into Christ, is facilitated when we strive to 'put on Christ' by embodying the attitudes which we learn through consistent reflection upon His life.

Attitudinal growth springs from the inner dimension of self. The shaping of attitudes requires a good bit of what Gabriel Marcel referred to as 'creative fidelity'. Notice the word, "creative". In the development of attitudes one cannot be passive. It is a fidelity in which I actively co-operate with God in the blossoming and fruition of my person-hood. The more we embrace 'the mind of Christ' the more we live from the deepest core of our being. We come to "significant being" with the help of grace. In a talk delivered at the Whitehouse Conference, Abraham Heschel remarked that it takes three things to attain this goal: "God, a soul, and a moment".[1] It is God Himself who fills us to overflowing with the fruits of the Spirit, life and peace, but for God it is always *the moment*—the NOW time!

Our life is enriched through the Incarnation. Because it was the will of the Father, Christ humbled Himself to share our humanity. With the coming of Christ, our lives may be rooted in the deeper dimensions of faith and love and we can agree with Heschel when he exclaims, "just to be is a blessing; just to live is holy"[2]

Through experience, we know that spiritual development does not always keep pace with biological development. We know, too that all of life's development is a mixture of joy and pain and it is these elements that often obscure the work of the spirit. Though the underlying spiritual movement, at the core of our being, is never completely silenced or stilled, it can become sluggish and all but completely lost.

The whole complexity of life springs from the conflict between the body and spirit, towards ascendency. Our fallen human nature has made it difficult to come to acknowledge the spirit as the authentic locus of life. We can't see it or touch it, so we tend to negate it. We are often confused in our search for truth. Dependence on the Sacred and the owning of our limitations become paramount problems for our ego-centered nature. But we are not predestined to maintain this warped attitude. Through the Incarnation of Christ, we have been brought to a radical transformation, an absolute re-birth of our spiritual being. Through Christ, we have inherited a new liberty, a new freedom. The deliverance from our enslavement is liberation on a plane of being which is gift, and liberation on a plane of action which is conquest.[3] The essence of liberation as gift, is the transforming of the very roots of our liberty, thus enabling us to see clearly. Through this liberation light is conferred upon us and the hidden and un-mined divine realities come into view. The gift is primarily one of vision such that the outlook and mind of Christ is grafted upon our own. This was the import of Christ's death and resurrection to bring us to new life. This is the heart of our belief.

Conquest of Self

A two-fold awareness comes to us through this restored vision. We realize that God calls us to eternal things and that through the Cross we are redeemed and introduced into the very life of God. Moroux concludes that we come to re-birth, through which we discover the divine aspect of our being and our vocation as spiritual creatures. As a spiritual creature, we understand the significance of struggle and effort in the slow re-conquest of the self. This unites us with Christ's sufferings but also with the power of the resurrection through which we may partake of Christ's glory. Imbued with the resurrection mysteries we are able to pass from our former ways to newness of life.

To be truly free, one must be master of the self. Our life must be so organized that the spirit rules the flesh. Grace is the power which masters the body and heals our spirit through the power of the Holy Spirit.

A further criterion of liberty is love. The Christian, animated by charity, loves God more than self. This love, which is also grace, frees us from selfish egoism and isolation as well as hardness of heart. Because we participate in the love of God, who **IS** immeasurable love, our inclinations are toward joy and hope. We are impelled toward more lofty desires and more exalted interests. In short, we come to the liberty of a child of God. The soul is implanted with a new seed of judgment, self-mastery and generosity but the splendid new planting demands voluntary action on our part. It was not God's plan to gift us with absolute, ready-made freedom. It was the Divine will, that through Redemption it was made possible for us to attain our personal liberty. It is as though Christ is saying to us, "The work of Redemption has been accomplished, yet all the work on your part, remains to be done. Become what thou art."

In this becoming, the conquest goes on. Ontologically, we are free, but psychologically and morally we have yet to attain fullness of liberty. St. Paul refers to this condition as one of slavery. Through Baptism, Christ came to dwell in our soul by grace. We truly have been freed from sin, yet we know little of the spontaneity and lightheartedness of the truly free spirit. Again and again we feel the tension of the incomplete. Just as often through striving and sincere commitment we overthrow the dominance of the 'body' self and make room for God at the level of our deepest center.

We question: "Is it possible for Christians to loosen the bonds which bind us—to come to wholeness?" We must believe! At its very heart, liberty is quickened by love and each act of faith makes it possible for spiritual liberty to strike deeper roots. Step by step the soul awakens to the dawning realization that to love is to obey the ordinances of our God, to renounce the self and to be united with the Beloved. Obedience gives way to communion. The soul responds (as far as it is humanly possible) to its most radical vocation—transformation in Christ.

In the biblical figure of Simeon, an upright man of careful observance, we can trace the two-fold movement of liberation as gift and as action, toward conquest. The person of Simeon is familiar to us from Scrpture.[4] Simeon stands at the threshold of Christianity and portrays an intense desire for the coming of Christ.

Long life and the precise historical setting of it, were gifts for Simeon. He could look back over the faithfulness of his many years and forward to the fulfillment of the Promise which he had received from the Holy Spirit that he should not see death "until he had seen the Christ, the anointed".[5] The gift of being in this particular time span enabled Simeon to witness the coming of Christ. From such a vantage point, Simeon became a man of extraordinary vision. Light was conferred upon him. For Simeon, this gift is realized in the poignant Temple scene when the old man recognized the Infant who is Himself the Light of the World. This experience was the crowning joy of Simeon's just and upright life.

The theme of conquest is apparent also in the Gospel narrative, though in the few lines presented there, this element is not so easily perceived. The contemporary poem, of T.S. Eliot, "A Song for Simeon", concretizes the conquest thread more clearly. Faithful to the theme of the Gospel and central to the unfolding in Eliot's poem is the waiting for the Lord and death. Simeon is an old man. He is "one of eighty years and no tomorrow."[6]

Eliot's poem begins with illusions to the fact that Jerusalem is under the foreign domination of Rome and that Simeon is longing to die. He speaks about the 'stubborn season making a stand' and the thread-like experience which Simeon is experiencing relative to his own life.

The lines of the poem seem to pivot on the statement: "The stubborn season has made a stand." In this context winter might be regarded as the "stubborn season". Winter holds tenaciously to its snow, reluctant to yield readily to spring. So too, Simeon in his old age, determined to see the fulfillment of the Promise, makes a stand. He shall not see death until his dimmed eyes have beheld the Christ Child. He will 'stubbornly' endure until the conquest is complete.

The second section of Eliot's poem has the ancient Simeon reflecting. Looking backward the old man remembers the steadfastness of his past and enjoys the consolation which a life animated by charity has afforded him. If as Mouroux says, a criterion of liberty is love, then we see it in Simeon, the free man. He remembers his life as one of faithfulness and giving. He recalls the many years in which he walked about the city looking for the poor and also welcoming them at his door.[7]

When the spirit dominates the flesh one is more apt to be open to God. As a result of this openness, Simeon is gifted with the ability to recognize the Infant, "the still unspeaking and unspoken Word."[8]

The last lines of the poem direct Simeon's thoughtfulness into the future. He muses that every generation shall praise this Child, and he speaks too, of the suffering to which all will be subjected who render this Child recognition. In Simeon we see love so rooted in the soul that it prompts a desire to be with the Beloved. Simeon had nothing more for which to live. Joyously he awaits death.

If we might characterize the life of Simeon in a word we might think of him as a watchman—one who kept the good watch. The little we know of Simeon embraces the fact that he waited daily at the Temple, watching carefully as people passed in and out that he might catch a glimpse of the Redeemer and ultimately hold Him in his aged arms.

To the uninformed observer Simeon's life may have appeared as the personification of idling or the epitome of a day-dream. Apparently accomplishing nothing, Simeon grew to a sense of being and fulfillment. His faithful watching at the door of the Temple was one of daily renewal in hope.

Simeon's physical life was marked off in chronological years, 'eighty and no tomorrow', but time for Simeon was opportunity. It was a "kairos" event. The characteristic circumstances of his life blended together to effect the joy of communion which he realized as he held the Child in his arms.

A Creative Tension

Time for me has both the elements of chronology and kairos. Day after day I add to the chronology of my life—but more than that, each day is opportunity—a kairos time. Time viewed merely as a matter of days and weeks becomes a limitation. Time viewed as an opportunity, challenges me to lead a meaningful life replete with struggle between the spirit and the flesh—a creative tension.

Each involvement of my day may become an act of faith in Him who has given me life and through whom I have been redeemed. The very act of Simeon's daily trip to the Temple was an implicit act of faith. He believed that what was promised him would be fulfilled. The realization that "I am alive in Christ" is an act of faith also. Living my life in harmony with this realization then, takes the dimension of conquest. Faith grows into love to such an extent that I strive to be 'oned' with the Beloved already on earth.

In the process of our becoming, there is need to become like Simeon. There is the aspect of waiting rather than doing. Sometimes we merely have to wait for the Lord to take the "first step" . . . to grace us with the knowledge we need at the moment, to touch the woundedness of ourselves so that we can cry out for mercy. At times we need to ask the Lord to make sweet the bitterness of our lives—to help us make sense of the things that do not seem to make any sense at all. We need to wait upon the Lord to break through with the courage we need to bear what seems to be unbearable . . . we wait for the darkness to dissipate and the fog to lift so we are able to see the LIGHT. Waiting can be a true prayer and authentic stance of the process of becoming.

The truth of our becoming is never really accomplished. So we continue the inward journey, and as Milton has the blind man poetically reflect, "He also serves who only stands and waits!" This was the 'service' Simeon rendered. Ponder how he was rewarded! Simeon's goal was attained and he could render his spirit peacefully back to the Child he held in his arms. In Simeon we see one whose entire life was enriched through the investment he made to surpass seeming odds. As Paul concludes in the letter to the Romans: "to live the life of nature is to think thoughts of nature; to live the life of the spirit is to think thoughts of the spirit: and natural wisdom brings only death whereas the wisdom of the spirit brings life and peace."[9]

M. GERMAINE HUSTEDDE, PHJC

NOTES:

1. Abraham J. Heschel, "The Older Person and the Family in the Perspective of the Jewish Tradition." (Paper presented at the Whitehouse Conference on Aging, Washington, D.C.), 1961.

2. Ibid.

3. Cf. Jean Moroux, The Meaning of Man, trans. A.H.G. Downes (New York: Sheed and Ward, 1952), pp. 175-186.

4. Cf. Luke, 2: 21-36.

5. Lk. 2:27.

6. Cf. T.S. Eliot, Selected Poems (New York: Harcourt, Brace and World, Inc., 1930) p. 99.

7. Ibid.

8. Ibid.

9. Romans 8: 5-6

CHARISM

COUNTER-POINT

SIMEON
Wreathed in tatters of age
 And Spirit-learned Wisdom
 Enfolds Salvation,
 The Anointed ONE-OF-GOD
 Sent in mercy.

 Blessing God
 His prayer pleads:

 "Let they servant go-
 My eyes have seen Thy LIGHT".

JESUS
Swaddled in infant weakness
Awaits the Spirit's timing . . .
A Sign to choose or refuse.

SIMEON: Journey ended
   JESUS: Mission begun.

FOR REFLECTION:

What makes it difficult for me to await the Spirit's timing?

Can I reflect peacefully upon the end of my journey and welcome it?

What is my specific mission in life at this time?

CHAPTER TEN

WITH MY LIFE, I THEE WORSHIP

LIVING CONSCIENTIOUSLY IN an aura of righteousness and love, can be a profound expression of worship! I worship the God who sustains me, the Christ who redeemed me and who showed me the way to live through example, and the Holy Spirit who sanctifies and enlightens me.

The gradual unfolding and my journey inward is, for the Christian, an unfolding and journey into Christ. Through the Incarnation, we are given a perfect example of our gradual unfolding and journey toward inwardness. But the tension we alluded to previously is ever present. The process by which we come to our most authentic self is replete with temptations. We can misuse the freedom that is ours and betray the gift that is given to us. We can be unfaithful to ourselves by failing to accept the truth of who I am, and thus abort the effort toward authentic becoming. Metz, in Poverty of Spirit says that the "categorical imperative of Christian life is the loving acceptance of the humanity which has been given us."[1] The embrace and loving acceptance of who I am is bound up with implicitly accepting the will of the Father for me. Acceptance of the self becomes concrete in the sometimes painful experience of everyday living. The experience of living contains the spiritual adventure of becoming an authentic self. We see this adventure unfolding in our Divine Model through the temptations of Christ in the wilderness.

The well known account of the temptations of Christ, by the Devil, possesses the spiritual lineaments of growth into humanness. Christ chose to redeem us through radical self-renunciation. God became man!

Just what does that mean for us? To become human means to become utterly poor. Metz, in his classic work says it is about having nothing which we might brag about before God. When we think about it—we have nothing which we did not receive from the loving hands of the Creator! He goes on to say that in our humanness we have no power or support of our own except the 'enthusiasm and commitment of [our] own heart.[2]

In becoming man, Jesus accepted this status. In the temptations of our Lord in the wilderness Satan tries to obstruct the perfect poverty of Jesus. Metz sees the temptations as an assault on the self-renunciation of God; an allurement to strength, security and spiritual abundance. Essentially, Satan tempts Jesus to cling to his divinity. He prefers God to remain simply God.

The devil's strategy is to get Jesus to betray his humanity. He tempts Jesus to change stones into bread, to cast himself from the temple and consequently to be ministered to by angels. Lastly, the devil tempts Jesus to sneak away from our abject condition of human poverty through acquisitions of kingdoms and glory.

The resounding "no" of Jesus to each of Satan's proposals was, at the same time, his embracing "yes" to our humanity. Jesus freely opted to immerse himself in our plight; to be hungry, to be subject to the laws of nature, to be forced to earn a living by the sweat of His brow. Jesus knew the loneliness and futility of the human existence to which he was exposing himself. He knew the gnawing hunger of every human being which can never be fully satiated. He knew our desire for security, power and self-fulfillment. Christ knew all this and yet he chose the full weight of our human existence and allowed himself to be tempted. Christ, the sinless One, reached the epitome of His poverty on Calvary. Bereft of companionship and consolation, the Son of God experienced seeming rejection by the heavenly Father. Stretched taut on the Cross, Jesus uttered the agonizing cry, "My God, my God why have You forsaken me?"[3] In His deepest self, Jesus experienced rejection and rebuff. "He came and stood with us, struggling with his whole heart to have us say 'yes' to our innate poverty".[4]

The concrete shapes of poverty in the life of Christ are also realities in our life. The human condition is inseparably connected with poverty—the poverty that results as deprivation because of our fall from original justice. It is a poverty unto death for we are finite beings. The minute we are born, we begin to die.

Through the Incarnation, Jesus became a limited, situated being-in-the-world, as well as a being-unto-death. Christ not only identified with our humanness, *He chose it* and expresses the reality of His choice in the way He lived among us.

The Poverty of My Unique Self

During the course of my life, I experience the poverty of my unique self. The limitations which bind me are characteristically mine. I may own each of them and find in them, a means to give praise and glory to the Father. On the other hand, to my detriment, I may attempt to overlook them, to rationalize about them or ignore them completely. Suppose, I am naturally given to be short tempered, irascible. Periodically, I find myself in difficulty because of this basic temperament. I may stoutly deny that I am given to ill temper. I may skirt the reality of my disposition by blaming anyone or anything in sight. Or I may inwardly seethe, yet outwardly refuse to acknowledge the "kettle' boiling within. On the other hand, I may heroically attempt to cope with my choleric disposition, but still fail frequently. The poverty of affability that I experience may bring me to the realization that, of myself, I am too weak to overcome the irascible bent of my disposition. There may be other forms of poverty that cause me pain. A person of lethargic temperament may find it extremely difficult to face the challenge of earning a living. Someone who is given to pride may bristle under the smallest slight. Discovering self is often a frightful territory that we are brought to explore. However, experiencing brokenness of any kind or description can fill me with anxiety, fear or resentment. But getting in touch with our own shadow is not all darkness. It is precisely here that we discover the beauty of our unique self. As St. Paul counsels us, it is when I am weak that I am strong! We begin to see the light and this prompts us too, to confide the truth of my being to the Lord and ask Him to be my strength.

My limitations make me different from everyone else, not in the sense that I alone have limitations, but in the sense that *my* limitations are *mine*, and not yours. My poverty is unique to me.

I may also experience the dynamics of poverty when I genuinely encounter another. I am called to empty myself of my prejudices, my preconceived ideas, biases, notions or opinions. I try to put away all traces of negativity in order to allow the uniqueness of the other to unfold. If I am closed to the mystery of the being of another, I can only encounter myself. I not only forfeit the possibility of worshipping the Lord by praising Him for this unique creation, I reduce myself to loneliness. I attempt to be filled at the parched and empty rivulet of the ego, while ignoring the rich and vast river of human personalities and experience.

Sometimes poverty is experienced in my life because of a need to stand alone. A certain value or ideal which I cherish may require the aloneness of standing on principle. You could probably name instances in your life when you felt isolated because others did not hold your treasured values or were fearful to make them known. As a Community, we experienced this individually and communally, when we felt called to do something for the many Leprosy patient beggars that lined the streets in front of our convent in India. The first affront came from the many government offices who thought we were trying to address a monumental problem and therefore were not initially very supportive. It was truly a lonely experience going from one official to another trying to obtain the necessary approbation to go ahead with the project.

The second, and even more distressing instance, was the reaction of the local citizenry when they became aware of the fact that we truly meant to build a Centre which would address Leprosy through early identification and control. We were picketed, harassed, maligned and insulted, not so much because we were their enemies, but because they did not really understand what we were trying to do. We did not back down, because the plight of these abject poor spoke to us and our charism—our commitment to the poor and marginalized of society.

In the early seventies, the disease of leprosy was rampant in India. Persons who suffered from Hansen's disease were outcasts, even as in the Lord's day. There was a very real fear, particularly among family members that the disease was highly contagious. So the streets were populated with these unfortunates. At night they huddled together in makeshift shelters. Come morning, they began their daily begging. Even for them to buy, or beg, food was "if-fy".

Because we weathered the aloneness, we succeeded in building the KKLCS (Katherine Kasper Leprosy Control Scheme) Centre. We had two main goals: To assist the easily identifiable patients we encountered everywhere and to educate the people about the truth of Leprosy. In the first instance we gathered patients from the street and engaged a very compassionate Indian doctor to assist in diagnosis, prescription medicine to keep patients from getting worse, supplying food, clothing and sometimes shelter. Very serious patients were transferred to a hospital in Tamil Nadu. Our friend, a stalwart lady Doctor Vomstein from Germany had practically single handedly built this oasis for the leprosy outcasts. Many reconstructive surgeries were done there. Imagine, a poor patient whose nose had been "eaten" away returning with a reconstructed nose! A modern day miracle!

You notice I have put the word *eaten* in quotes. The hands, feet, noses and earlobes are not really "eaten" by the disease of leprosy. The bacillus which causes the disease cannot live in the warm parts of the body, so it travels to the extremities. Attacking the nervous system, it renders the particular organ insensitive to touch. Thus, patients often end up with gangrenous wounds of secondary causes since they feel no pain. Gradually, the hand, foot or nose disappears because of this concomitant factor.

Our second goal was addressed through early detection of the disease. Our Team visited schools, factories, public gatherings of any sort, to give free check-ups. An educational film was shot to teach the truth about leprosy that people had so long been denied them. After sometime we did not have to go out looking for patients; they came to us voluntarily. Always, the concern was a scaly, white spot which very often indicated the earliest stages of the disease. With proper medication and regular monitoring it could be controlled. By the grace of God and a willingness to bear a certain loneliness, the incidence of Leprosy in our locality in India has dramatically decreased. We cannot say that we made all the difference, but we did a lot to raise people's consciousness. The first great step toward any change is awareness.

Supporting any value in the face of opposition or indifference may be a source of aloneness. It would perhaps be much easier just to ignore the situation. However, deep inside one's self, we know that to compromise would betray something very precious and important to us. So, we choose to stand alone and suffer the death of loneliness. We know this poverty is part of the price which coming to true selfhood demands.

Poverty of the Commonplace

Another source of poverty may be the uneventful common everyday existence which is my lot. Life for the most part has no special fan-fare about it. It is commonplace, simple. The extraordinary is the unusual. The way in which I am present to the simple and commonplace makes the difference. Tagore highlights the poverty of the commonplace and the embrace of it that gives way to a precious contradistinction. In his mature age he had a responsible work is various villages. He spoke of the 'current of time' which meandered slowly and contained its shades of light and dark. Most of his days, in his words, were filled with 'drifting trivialities.' One day as his work was completed he went down to the river to take his bath. He stood for some moments welcoming the spring rain. Then he felt a conscious stirring of his soul within him. In that moment things which previously had not made any sense or were 'detached and dim' came together with a great sense of unity and meaning. He says that the feeling which he had at that moment was like that of someone who had been groping through the fog and 'suddenly discovers that he stands before his own house'.[5]

Probably, most of us could say that our day is a succession of 'drifting trivialities' yet in the everyday, moments of light and relaxation are present. Occasionally, the common ordinary gives way to something special. Why this change? Tagore tells us how he paused momentarily to welcome the commonplace. He became "conscious of a stirring within" himself. All that had gone before seemed to melt into a kind of unity. A new meaning arose from the simplicity of the everyday. Tagore experienced a strange new feeling of "at-home-ness" within himself.

How often do we live as strangers within our own skin? If I feel alien and dissatisfied in my everyday experience perhaps it is because I fail to appreciate my surroundings. Perhaps I never slow down sufficiently to acknowledge the fullness of my day and therefore I find it empty. I may rebel against the concrete poverty of my mundane experience. If I have allowed my everyday life to degenerate into sterile routine, I may yearn and search for the different, the impressive, rather than embrace the poverty of my situatedness.

The last expression of Christ's poverty came at the end of his life when he faced the bitter passion and death. This was the moment of attainment of perfect humanity. Unlike Christ, I come to death still striving for full humanness. Striving toward, but never quite attaining the goal of complete self-actualization, is an expression of my basic poverty–my humanness! At the very heart of human poverty is a lifetime of paradoxes: joys and sorrows, losses and gains, potential and limitations, growth and diminishment, life and death. The spirit of poverty, then, might be summarized as the acceptance of the rhythms of life which parallel my radical humanness.

Negatively, poverty may include any aspect of my life in which I suffer want. Physically, I may lack certain gifts and abilities I would very much like to possess. I may be woefully wanting in musical talent or the ability to compete in sports. On the psychological level I may find that I am timid and shy. Spiritually, there may be the implicit hunger that I feel for the Infinite. I am never completely satisfied. From a positive point of view I may accept myself just as I am and give praise and thanks to the gracious God for all the gifts I *do* have and try to be the best that I can be.

In my active, work oriented existence, it is rather simple to disregard the poor person that I am. I manage to substitute some accomplishment or some pleasant experience to dull the edge of my insufficiency, to conceal my limitations. As long as I find someone or something to compensate for the lack or void I feel, I never allow the true state of my poverty to surface. My life resembles the childhood game of "Blind Man's Bluff". I may think that I am serious about the signals of life but these same signals beckoning me to authentic living are weak and the reception is poor. I fail to identify the obstacles. I remain a stranger to myself.

Being caught in instances of separation and loss can also put me in touch with my radical poverty. Heidegger[6] makes the poignant observation that as soon as one comes to life, one is old enough to die. He says that 'being-toward-death' essentially identifies us, but this same identification possesses also the phenomenon of coming to self-hood. He says that we mistakenly regard death as the moment which does drastic violence to life, whereas in actuality, death is the essence of life. Our attitude toward dying gives us information about the life that we live. Authentic living embraces the poverty of death and discloses one of the most identifying marks of our finitude. This thought should orient us toward our ultimate end, but also stimulate a kind of urgency and responsibility in living.

Through the example of Christ we learn to cope with our poverty. My self-experiences incorporate the mysterious blend of the body-ego-spirit that I am. I realize that I am never perfect, never completely satisfied, never fully realized on any level of my humanness. Above all, my poverty is an opportunity to make an act of faith in the love of God, who created me, sustains me and buoys me up in my every endeavor. Such is His embracing tenderness, His constant love and fidelity.

NOTES

1. Johannes B. Metz, <u>Poverty of Spirit</u>, Trans. John Drury (Paramus, N.J.: Newman Press, 1968), pp. 5-20.

2. Cf. Metz, <u>Op. Cit.</u>, p. 14.

3. Matt. 27: 46.

4. Metz., <u>Op. Cit</u>., p.19

5. Cf. Rabindranath Tagore, <u>The Religion of Man</u> (Boston: Beacon Press Paperback, 1961), pp.94-95.

6. Cf. Martin Heidegger, <u>Being and Time</u>, Trans. John Macquarrie and Edward Robinson (London: SCM Press, Ltd., 1962) p. 279 ff.

OIL AND INCENSE

DESIRE'S ANOINTNG

I, too, would anoint Thee, Lord,
With fragrant, unctuous, precious nard.
Desire alone, do I possess—
The costly balm, not my bequest.

Be I so poor, bereft, unfree—
I've nothing with to worship Thee?

Instinctively, I gather oil,
Pressed from the grind of daily toil.
Nectar, of my garden flowers,
Juices of emotion's powers.
The dew of morning meadow strewn
And solitude's choicest, rare perfume.

Ah true! No jardinière have I
Replete
With ointment for thy feet!

Yet, bring I all my heart's desire,
To place upon the blazing pyre.
As incense furls and prayers unfold
I worship Thee as Magdalene of old.

M. GERMAINE HUSTEDDE, PHJC

FOR REFLECTION:

When have I had the experience of pressing precious oil for worship from my daily toil?

What rare perfume have I experienced in solitude?

Name the poverties that irritate me the most. How can I change them into offerings for worship?

CHAPTER ELEVEN

WEAVING THE MANTLE

TO THE EXTENT that I can let go of pre-conceived notions, ideas and ideals about God, and myself, to that extent will I grow into the Spirit of Christ. Careful reading and reflection of the Gospel provides myriad possibilities for encountering Christ and these establish the pattern for me to follow. There is 'reading' and 'reading' of the Scriptures! A weighted, exegetical approach which tends to analytical interpretation may cloud my vision. Intellectually, I may store up all sorts of knowledge but profit little in my attempt to allow Christ to be a pattern for me. Christ is at one and the same time, the right measure of belief and faith in God, but also the right measure for my daily living. One needs to look no further. Christ is the perfect pattern, which pattern is not easily discovered through cursory reading of Scripture. Daily living patterned after Christ evidences an existential realization of what following Him means. When Christ chose the disciples, Scriptures tells us that he chose them to 'be with him and to be sent". The 'being with' is the locus of learning and really getting to know Jesus in a personal way. It is pre-requisite to 'being sent'.

According to Kierkegaard[1] perseverance in discerning the pattern delineated by Christ, and appropriating it into one's life style, results in presence. Thus, an internalization takes place whereby the seeker experiences a personal encounter, and becomes a modern day disciple. The authentic spirit of Jesus becomes more and more embodied in one's daily existence.

The basic axiom consists in the fact that the would-be Christian must shape one's life according to the precepts and commands of Jesus. "Limited commitment is no commitment; purity of heart is to will one thing wholly and at all times."[2] Total commitment to Christ eventually effects a radical transformation in one's self. The Christian becomes more alive to Christ and dead to the world, its pursuits and pleasures. The Christian labors unceasingly to minimize these influences. The elements of constancy and intensity are the framework of the "narrow door" which leads to Life.

One's entire life may be described as "striving toward" wholeness since complete attainment of the goal is impossible for our fallen human nature. The Christian quest therefore, takes on the unending process of becoming. Kierkegaard aptly notes that "one is not enrolled in the mantle of following" in one sweeping gesture. He says that the follower must 'earn' this status "thread by thread". The final conclusion is that we are always becoming—always on the way. We are pilgrim people![3]

Since the follower of Christ can only approximate the pattern in weaving the mantle of wholeness and holiness, the only recourse is to accept, and own, one's deficiencies. All along the path of 'following'—from start to finish—grace is present and plentiful for the needs of the pilgrim. It behooves us to rely on the ever-present gracious of our God.

If I was born into a Christian family and tradition, it may happen that I find myself in the footsteps of Christ through mild force or mere routine. Perhaps I am keeping step from motives of human respect. As I grew older, I may recognize that my following of Christ has overtones of moralism. I have convinced myself that as long as I do the 'right thing' I am following Christ. This could lead me to the hope of "self-salvation" by placing my trust in the false security of legalism. It reminds me of Eliot's impressive couplet in which he says that it is the greatest treason to do the right thing for the wrong reason.[4]

The Heart of the Matter

Motivation, along these lines, never really gets to the heart of the matter. The pristine, authentic motivation for following Christ springs from a heart overflowing with gratitude for all that Christ has done and continues to do for me, day by day. I find Christ as the paradigm for my life. I reflect on passages of Scripture, especially those of the New Testament, and find concretely the threads necessary for me to weave the mantle of holiness; to put on Christ.

The meeting of Christ in Scripture must engage me more than just on an intellectual level. I cannot really meet Christ, or encounter Him in Scripture, if I approach the Sacred Text with an analytical stance. The meeting of Christ in Scripture and discerning the art of choosing the threads, and weaving the mantle, requires my full attention and commitment. It is a matter of the heart! My faith response amounts to my personal encounter with a personal God. A true encounter of Christ in Scripture is a meeting of two persons: Christ and myself. It engenders a "phenomenon of communion."[5] This means that I must attempt to personalize the virtues and values I find in Christ. Reflective, prayerful reading of Scripture ought to be in the service of my daily spiritual living and in the fashioning of an ever deeper bond with Christ in commitment, love and fidelity.

There is a dynamic of call and response in Luke's gospel. In fact, it is a theme that runs throughout the entire Old and New Testaments. Again and again God calls certain individuals to serve as prophet, emissary, messenger, apostle or Mother of God. Much of salvation history is dependent upon this rhythm.

The same rhythm runs through the lives of every human being, though perhaps not so dramatically. I could consider my initial call as a call into being—the springboard which projects me into every ensuing summons. It is in the rhythm of call/response that I weave the mantle of my unique individuality. At our birth one may truly say all is shrouded in mystery. This mode, however, continues all through life. I cannot know what the future will be. But we do know that each person is called ultimately to some dedicated or consecrated future.

Our potentiality to be called derives from the fundamental structure of ourselves as religious, i.e., persons with the ability to be called beyond ourselves, to transcend our human, daily bondedness and to acknowledge the Holy. Each person's call is unique. The voice of the Eternal in the very depths of my being beckons me to respond with the whole of myself.

When we speak of life-call we are not referring to some profession: doctor, lawyer, dentist, home-maker. These are avocations which unfold in the course of life, sometimes parallel with one's life call. These invitations point to my ability to be called and from time to time bring me to the awareness that I am *being called upon* in the service of another. These are partial invitations which can be related to my eternal call in the sense that everything in my life can be related to the harmonious unfolding of one's life call.

In contrast to a partial invitation, a life call is described as "the call to consecrate my life in a total, final and transcendent way to the sacred, within one or other fundamental life form, such as marriage, the single state or religious life."[6] Life embraces the possibility of many invitations but generally only one life call.

One call in life emerges more forcefully and deeply than the all the others. It is the call which urges me to embrace one or the other fundamental lasting life form. Adolescence is usually the ante-chamber to commitment of oneself to a particular, fundamental life form. A youth begins to experience a mysterious tending toward one specific life form. Life-form is different from life-call but it is a fundamental expression of it. Emerging self-awareness awakens me to experience my life as my responsibility. I feel myself called to be realized in a unique way in both human and spiritual dimensions. I feel an urge to make my life worthwhile. But I may also be overwhelmed by the awesome reality that my life is in my hands. If I do not heed what I am convinced is my life-call, I am bound to experience a deep sense of guilt which surges up from the core of my being. I experience a sense of betraying myself or of wasting my life.

The experience of life-guilt may be a grace or blessing for it prods me to return to the sincere pursuit of my life-call and to regain a sense of responsibility toward my life as a whole. The great Exemplar of the life-call is Christ whose entire life was permeated and directed by a concern for the will of the Father.

The life of each individual is a time bound, concrete situational series of events in which I am called to participate. From the human perspective there is a certain indefiniteness which characterizes my life-call as a whole. I may not always be able to understand what happens to me, but in faith I accept every incident as an expression of my life-call. We cannot fully define it because to be human is to be open to the mystery that I am as well as to the element of surprise.

The unfolding of my life is a mystery. Even at this moment I do not know how the Divine plan of God will be articulated in my regard, yet, I have experienced that the events, encounters and experiences of my past do fit together like so many pieces of a giant jig-saw puzzle. Hindsight seems to be the enlightening factor. This is true for all the years I have lived, but there are still empty spaces in the puzzle of life. The future contains all the missing pieces!

It is important too, to remember that each specific life-form has inherent limitations which characterize it and distinguish one form from another. The response to a particular life-form opens me to some possibilities and closes me to others. For example, the religious life-form may provide special opportunities for recollection, prayerfulness or ministry as a missionary in the course of my unfolding. However, if I embrace religious life, I have fewer opportunities for social engagement. The limited and limiting aspects are part of the acceptance of a particular life-form and are best overcome when I am able to concentrate on the positive aspects and accentuate them.

Charles de Foucauld and Life-Call

To help us understand well the mystery of life-call, we need to reflect on the life of someone full spent, to see how the patterns of life-call come together. The biography of Charles de Foucauld will exemplify this.

Charles was born on September 15, 1858. As a small boy, Charles appeared headstrong and stubbornly self-centered. His father was a nervous, high strung man of ill health who was away much of the time. Charles remembered him vaguely. His mother was a pious woman and from her, Charles absorbed whatever piety permeated his youth.

Mme. De Foucauld died at the age of thirty four. A few months after the death of his wife, the ailing father died bequeathing to young Charles the title Viscount de Foucauld of Frontbriand. The boy and his sister, Marie, were adopted by the maternal grandfather and his second wife. This turn of events succeeded in spoiling the headstrong lad even further. The indulgent old grandfather considered Charles' display of temper a sign of character.

At fourteen Charles received his first Communion at Nancy Cathedral in France. At this time, he also entered the Nancy Lycée which had become renowned for shaping illustrious men. At first Charles was an average student with average grades. Soon, however, he was overwhelmed by his love of leisure. Reason triumphed over religion and the erotic over the erudite. Somehow Charles managed to graduate at the age of sixteen.

After graduation, Charles was summoned by his grandfather. "Charles" said the grandfather, "you have come to the crossroads. You must decide what you want to become as a man." Charles was undecided and everything grandfather suggested seemed too demanding to lazy Charles. Because of grandfather's insistence that he decide upon something, Charles finally decided upon a career in the army. He was to prepare to enroll in the Jesuit school of St. Genevieve in Paris which would ready him for his entrance into Saint-Cyr, the West Point of France.

Charles hated school. He even found Paris strange and unattractive, except for its luxuries! He no longer believed in God. Later Charles characterized this time of his youth saying that it was all selfishness, vanity and irreverence consumed by a desire for evil.[7] Charles was seventeen at the time and completely disoriented in his life.

Barely passing the entrance exams for Saint-Cyr, Charles managed to coast along for two years and graduated 333rd in a class of 386. The elderly grandfather was spared this humiliation, for the old colonel had died, bequeathing the young Viscount 84,000 gold francs. Charles was twenty-one.

Now, rich, spoiled and irresponsible, Charles indulged in even more loose living. He became a lavish spender and gambled incessantly. He made Mimi, a girl of his fancy, "a highly ornamental focus for an otherwise empty and aimless life."[8] Having tasted all the worldly pleasure that France had to offer, he was glad to be sent to Africa with his regiment. Africa, with its Moslems, held a fascination for Charles. He was impressed by the blind religious faith of the Moslems and seduced by a spell which the 'Dark Continent' cast upon him. Still, the headstrong, ego-oriented dimension of his self prevailed. As a result, Charles was placed on the inactive service list because of insubordination and conduct unbecoming an officer and a gentleman.

Up until this time Charles' life had been dissipated and fragmented. His energies were directed after will-o'-the-wisps. Now back in France he followed the advance of his former regiment with keen interest. As he thought of his comrades riding into battle he knew that the army was more than discipline and routine. "The army was really a means of expression for a man who loved France, and who would push his love to the point of sacrifice"[9] Charles decided that the army would be a good place to find out if he was meant to be a real soldier in the highest sense of the word. Setting foot on African soil a second time gave Foucauld a sense of homecoming. The undisciplined cadet became a bold leader of men. A transformation began to take place in the desultory young officer.

One day as Foucauld and his troops returned from a reconnaissance mission, his men were jumped by a band of snipers. The skirmish lasted nearly half an hour. Foucauld was forced to call for fresh ammunition and supplies. There was no response from his Arab troops. Infuriated by his men's desertion, Foucauld finally galloped to the rear to berate such cowardly conduct, only to find his men prostrating themselves in prayer. The snipers, too, had stopped fighting. It was the moment of sunset and time for the Arabs to turn toward Mecca and proclaim the greatness of Allah.

In the silence that filled the wadi, Foucauld remembered the awesome quiet of the Cathedral of Nancy. He was reminded of his boyhood days when he still believed in God. Then that silence had meant that he was in the presence of God. In his adolescence he had laughed at such mawkish belief. He did not laugh now. The Arabs took God seriously.

After Foucauld's tour of duty, he undertook a dangerous mission to Morocco in the interest of exploring and mapping the vast desert land about which little was known. In the loneliness of the desert, Charles pondered his destiny. The spell of the African desert was in his blood. He would return there again.

June of 1884 saw Charles again in France. In July he fell seriously ill with a strange disease diagnosed as "mucous fever". This incapacitated him well into September. Autumn found Charles back in Algiers working had on the writing of his book, the compilation of the data he had uncovered on his Moroccan adventure. He was also seriously thinking of marriage. Mlle. Titre, the daughter of a retired army officer, stepped into Charles' life quite by accident. Charles had sought out the major, a noted geographer, to discuss some maps with him. As the two men talked the lovely lady came into the room. In her, Charles saw the "incarnation of love he had been seeking all his life . . . Here was peace and security for life. Here was a happy end to all his restlessness."[10] Charles asked the geographer for his daughter's hand and set about wooing her. He gave no inkling of this romance to his family but when he returned home in December and let the family in on his plans, he was surprised to find that they were not pleased. Charles was going to dilute the de Foucauld line, by marrying a plebian. Charles' stubbornness had once more been aroused. Nothing would stop him from marrying Mlle.Titre!

A cousin, Marie de Bondy, whom Charles had always been fond of, had a long chat with him. Before the evening had ended Marie helped Charles to see how unfair it would be to someone he really loved if he intended to pursue his travels to Morocco, the Sahara, the salt marshes of Tunisia, the Congo, Madagascar and who knew where, in the continent of Africa. Charles sat silently for a while. Then he smiled broadly. "You talk as if you would like me to become a monk," he said. Marie smiled, "Well, why not?" she responded.

Charles returned to Algiers but he did not see Mlle. Titre again. Instead, he explained to the major and withdrew his offer of marriage.

While many partial calls had invaded the life of de Foucauld, he still felt a restless uncertainty, a floundering about in his life. He had destroyed the faith he had as a youth; now it eluded him. As much as he sought the light, he could not find it. He returned to France and lived just a few doors from his Aunt Ines. His was a bachelor's existence. In his restless searching he used to frequent a quiet church not far from where he lived. "If thou art my God," he would pray, "make Thyself known to me, O Lord."[11]

Charles anguished through the long months, praying and searching, until one morning in late October, he rose early and sauntered into the church he often visited, the Plaće Saint-Augustin. He went directly to the confessional of Abbé Huvelin. In a standing position he told the Abbé he had no faith and he asked that he would teach him. "Kneel", ordered the priest, "and confess your sins to God and you will believe." Charles protested that he had not come for that purpose but at the Abbé's kind persistence he made a confession of all his sordid past. Charles walked from the confessional a little dazed but with a light and buoyant step. On that day he made what he called his "second first communion"[12] It was a turning point in his life. Charles felt himself a new man. The great weight of imperfection and sin no longer felt so overwhelming. Yet Charles searched for the life form he was to embrace. Two years to the day from the morning that he knelt in the Abbé's confessional, Charles sought out his spiritual guide once again. "Father, he said," I should like to dedicate my life to God." The Abbé shook his head and said, "You are not yet prepared my son. You cannot be sure."[12]

At the Abbé's suggestion, Foucauld made a pilgrimage to the Holy Land to pray and discern this important decision. When Charles returned, he had made four separate retreats, each in a different monastery to determine where God was calling him. He finally decided that God was calling him to the Trappist order. Charles was thirty-two.

The five years of Charles' Trappist life were restless. In a sense he found extreme poverty, renunciation and solitude, but for Charles this was not enough. He was loathe to half-measures. He wanted to come as close to the suffering of Jesus as possible. During this time, Charles conceived the idea of founding the Little Brothers of Jesus. He knew that he would never, in essence, be able to take final vows as a Trappist monk. In 1897, no longer bound by Trappist vows he secured passage aboard a steamer and was off again to the Holy Land. He bound himself, however, by personal vow to perpetual chastity and poverty.

After three years as a handy man for the Poor Clares in Nazareth, Charles felt called to return to his native France. He visited briefly with this spiritual director, Abbé Huvelin and discussed his desire to be ordained. This was what the old Abbé had in mind for Charles right from the beginning. With the Abbé's help Charles was off again, this time to Rome to study theology. On June 9th, 1901, at the age of forty-two, Charles was ordained at Vivieres.

France and the Holy Land had plenty of priests to serve the people's needs. Morocco, a country as large as France, with twelve million inhabitants, had not one single priest. In all of the Sahara there were perhaps a dozen missionaries. In order to procure the necessary permission for more quickly returning to Africa, Fr. Foucauld offered his services as an army chaplain to one of the French garrisons in Africa that was without a priest. Just outside the army compound of Beni-Abbes, Fr. Foucauld built the first little chapel on African soil. He planted a small garden and constructed a few extra buildings which were to be cells for the Little Brothers who never came. There was one room larger than all the rest. This was to be used for the passing traveler. From this spot, Charles served the needs of the soldiers in the area.

Several times he was called from his hermitage to traverse the vast desert in search of men who needed God. After a gypsy year of missionary travel in the Sahara, Brother Charles of Jesus, as he now called himself, decided that Beni-Abbes was home. He was not to stay here long however, for other parts of Africa beckoned him. Though he was always near to an army outpost that he might serve the needs of the soldiers, Foucauld did not limit his work to French soldiers.

The Hoggar country of the Tuareg people fascinated him. The Hoggar Highlands were finally to become Foucauld's parish. He chose the district of Tamanrasset in which to settle. It was a forsaken place, but one of stark beauty. His days were filled with prayer, silence, solitude and work. To make friends with the Tuareg people whom he visited frequently and presented small gifts, he worked diligently on a French-Tamashek dictionary. He also made a collection of Tamashek folklore and worked assiduously at translating the Scripture into the native language of the people.

Brother Charles was alone. He didn't mind the loneliness; it was part of the self-abnegation he had chosen. It was part of the mortification he had sought, but the years were speeding by and there was not a single kindred soul to nourish the seed he was planting. Charles was now forty-eight. He made requests of Bishops, the Trappists and even Abbé Huvelin to find someone who might be interested, but no one ever came.

The prejudice, aversion and mistrust of the Moslems were slow to dissipate. They could not understand the goodness and generosity of the Christian Marabout because Foucauld would not even be able to receive his proper reward. Charles could not go to heaven, they believed, because he was not a Moslem.

To accommodate his nomadic people, Brother Charles would move his "parish" when the Tuareg moved their flocks. Sometimes, this entailed hundreds of miles of travel. Asekrem, a good feeding ground in the summer was a breathtakingly beautiful country and a fitting place to worship the Creator.

In his last stay at Asekrem, Father Foucauld wrote a new will. In it he stipulated that he be buried in the exact spot where he died without shroud or coffin. His grave should be marked by a simple wooden cross. His motto read, as it had for the last twenty years, "Live today as though you were to die a martyr."[13]

When the great war of 1914 broke out in Europe, the ominous winds and unrest penetrated even to the desert of Africa. Father Charles feared for his people though he never revealed his concern. The Senuis, renegades, who were in sympathy with Germany, were attacking everywhere. At this time Foucauld wrote in his diary, "How kind is the good Lord to conceal the future from us. What torture we would hold if we were granted a glimpse of the unknown."[14]

On December 1, 1916, at the hands of some of the people he loved and for whom he had sacrificed himself, Father Foucauld died at the hands of an assassin's bullet. In all his years among the African people, Father had not made a single convert. He looked upon himself as 'the grain of wheat'; the harvest would come much later.

We can see from the life of Foucauld that he responded to the ever-present life-call. Charles' life unfolded in mystery and he frequently had to bow in faith and accept what was happening in his life as an articulation of his life call, though he never understood it.

The life-form which Foucauld finally chose was in response to an innate predisposition to silence, solitude, austerity and self-abnegation that surfaced only when he had quieted himself long enough to listen to the call of the Lord. The fundamental openness to the Holy that Charles was is revealed in his many prayerful, but painful moments of searching.

Life-form—a Life of Love

As we have seen in the life of Foucauld, the religious life-form is a life of love. It took on an ever deepening meaning through his life of service. Until his death, his life was a dynamic, vibrant, value-oriented existence. Daily he renewed his dedication to the life-call that God had shown him through the Holy Spirit. Through it he was transformed!

Daily life serves either as a means of transformation or disfiguration in my growth toward God and in companioning with the Holy Other. I have only one life to offer as proof of my love and gratitude. Though my life embraces the proverbial "ups and downs" as did that of Foucauld, it is not so different from that of Jesus, though Jesus was without sin. Nearly every page of Scripture highlights rhythms of disappointment, joy, and prejudice and acceptance, etc., which Christ experienced throughout his earthly life. Merely noting these brings little fuel to my furnace of love. I need to look beyond the incident portrayed to see how Christ responded to the situation and then attempt to pattern the garment of my life on His.

Christ's life was totally attuned to the will of the Father. Each thought, word, action and desire was in perfect conformity with the Father's will. Christ was able to use everything in His life as a link which bound Him to the Father. Here we experience the 'phenomenon of communion'. It is the intimacy which we all seek.

Because of the marvelous unity, body-soul-spirit, that we are, we can transcend time and space and cross over into the very presence of God. Though the awareness of God in my life can never be perfect because of my fallen humanness, I gently and calmly try to weave everything that happens in my life together with God's loving providence. In reality, the choices I make appropriate freedom or slavery to me.

Notes:

1. Cf. Bradley R. Dewey, <u>The New Obedience: Kirkegaard on Imitating Christ</u> (Washington, D.C.: Corpus Books,1968). pp. 119-161

2. Dewey, <u>Op. Cit.,</u> p 140.

3. Dewey, <u>Op. Cit.,</u> p. 152

4. TS. Eliot<u>, Murder in the Cathedral</u> (New York: Harcourt, Brace and World, Inc., 1935) p. 44.

5. Cf. Jean Moroux, <u>I Believe: The Personal Structure of Faith,</u> trans. Michael Turner (New York: Sheed and Ward, 1959) p.43.

6. Adrian van Kaam, <u>The Vowed Life</u> (Denville, New Jersey: Dimension Books, 1968), p 84.

7. Note: Much of the material, presented in this Chapter, is the inspiration of van Kaam's writings or unpublished class notes.

8. Marion Mill Preminger. <u>The Sands of Tamanrasset: the Story of Charles de Foucauld</u> (New York: Hawthorn Books Inc., 1961) p.23. Preminger, <u>Op. cit.,</u> P. 36.

9. <u>Ibid.,</u> p. 48.

10. <u>Ibid.,</u> p. 77.

11. <u>Ibid.,</u> p. 86.

12. <u>Ibid.,</u> p. 87.

13. Preminger, <u>Op. cit.,</u> p. 227

14. <u>Ibid.,</u> p. 238.

Further works which compliment the theme explored above are *Commitment to Christian Maturity* and *Divine Guidance*. Both are co-authored by Adrian van Kaam and Susan A. Muto.

Available at Epiphany Books /Pittsburg, PA.

NEW LIFE

WHICH WAY?

Which is the way to the dwelling place of LIGHT?
Do I follow a star, a comet or the moon?
Is the orbit of the sun from daybreak to dusk,
the way to consummate brightness?
How do I reach the dwelling place
of Him who lives in unapproachable light?

The path is clearly marked: ABANDON!
Abandon yourself to the ONE who is THE WAY.
He is the beginning and the end of the journey.
He is the Alpha and the Omega
He is TRUTH!
All deceit and personal striving
give way to the ONE who is LIFE
and LIGHT!

FOR REFLECTION:

What gifts characterize my life-call? Where is God calling me?

Does "ABANDON" seem too powerful a word to mark the path of following?

What forms of deceit and personal striving might still lurk in my spirit?

CHAPTER TWELVE

INTO LIBERTY

TOO OFTEN, I am my own worst enemy. The shackles that imprison me are undoubtedly forged by the same self that longs to be free. Paul, writing to Timothy, names the bonds that bind even the best of us.[1] Interestingly, he lists 'being in love with self' as the prime source of our slavery. Then all the other distortions follow and distract us from our goal. He concludes that there is no holiness without renunciation and spiritual warfare. All spiritual progress entails ascesis (mortification) as a way of self mastery which gradually leads to living in the joy and peace of the beatitudes.

Ontologically, we are free, but psychologically and morally, we have yet to attain the fullness of liberty. St. Paul refers to this condition as one of slavery. Through Baptism, Christ dwells in our souls by grace. God makes a home in us! How awesome! Initially, therefore we have been freed from sin, yet we know little of the spontaneity and lightheartedness of the truly free spirit. Proud egoism and base sensuality war against the spirit. Conversely, the spirit struggles and 'wars' against the flesh, for the spirit has been enlightened and visited in love. Again and again we experience the tension of the opposites!

Loosening the Bonds

It is possible for us to daily loosen the bonds which bind us—to come to wholeness. The essence of spirit is the power of knowing, or comprehending, that I am made for eternity. We find ourselves drawn toward the Infinite Spirit. This is a mystery and mastery which we can never exhaust. Because I innately realize that I am made for eternity, I come to know, too, that I am a being divinely called, and I must respond to that call. I simply cannot endure as a 'being' posited in the world. I must augment and fulfill my being through a radical law of action which demands that we both *possess* and *give* of ourselves. Possession is gained through self-awareness and self-mastery, while giving is forged though communion and love.

In our response to 'the call', the struggle for liberty is implied since the conquest of the self is at stake. Moroux says to possess one's self one must strive for self-mastery through an 'inexorable purification' of our animal tendencies. He urges us too, to break down obstacles and barriers that lurk in the dark corners of our spirit and to be so in possession of self that we finally find our self by 'ceasing to seek'[2]

Because I am endowed with free will, I am at liberty to choose my response. But respond, I must, in one way or another! The call-response dynamism constitutes my fundamental vocation–the integration of body-soul-spirit to the most perfect degree. Sometimes the response may be pure and joyous, coinciding with the potent call of self-conquest. Sometimes the response may be that of a timorous soul shrinking from the risk and sacrifice demanded and devoid of courage. The response could also take the form of wrestling between good and evil. The question is, do I attempt to realize myself as I *want* myself to be, or as I am *called* to be?

There are two faces of liberty here. In the first instance liberty takes the appearance of an attempt to realize one's self utterly independent of the transcendent call. In the latter instance, liberty is realized in giving oneself over to something greater and larger than the self. In the first attempt pseudo-liberty only dissipates and crumbles one's life for it is an attempt to come to wholeness while losing sight of the Whole. This ignores the principle of unity.

In place of mere dissipation, distorted liberty may take the form of some defined value while still refusing the transcendent value. This attitude stifles the spiritual energies and confines them to the realm of the human. The insidious problem here is that, for the unreflective person, the refusal of true liberty may pass unseen. Instead of committing self to something beyond self, I may opt for a way of service and allow doing or duty to take on the proportion of an absolute value. I could also invest my life with idealistic meaning. On the other hand, when I hear the call from the very core of my being, I give myself to Him in whom alone is found the ultimate foundation of duty and the realization of the absolute ideal.

Originality—Well-spring of Gifts

Moroux points out that in the way of service, the form which the gifts take are each different but the spiritual impulse which prompts each is of the same nature—a tendency to surpass the self.[3] When one attempts to put Moroux's theory into the context of life, spiritual liberty and freedom take on vivid meaning. A reflective reading of Gandhi's biography[4] indicates how his life unfolded in accord with his own unique and precious givenness—his originality. In essence such unfolding is the liberty and freedom of graceful living whether one lives to be an octogenarian or is called by death when one has briefly lived.

Gandhi's youth is unmarked by any outstanding characteristics. He was not particularly bright and displayed no great aptitude for learning. He was extremely shy and used to run home from classes as fast as he could for fear someone might wish to speak to him.

Some Indian plays Gandhi saw as a youth made a great impression on him. One in particular, the story of Harishchandra, an ancient king, who sacrificed and suffered greatly for the sake of truth, took root in Gandhi's deepest self. The impression which this tale made upon his youthful mind and spirit was never to be effaced. He used to re-enact the play for himself questioning, "Why should not all be truthful like Harishchandra?"

Gandhi's mother was a deeply religious woman. Her fasting and discipline did not go unnoticed to the observant Gandhi. However, the example of his mother was largely unheeded, as Gandhi himself confesses to the sins of his youth: meat-eating, smoking, lust, possessiveness and jealousy. When Gandhi learned that his meat-eating ventures were leading him into telling lies to his parents he decided to abstain from meat that he might safeguard the truth. Truth became an invaluable possession for Gandhi.

As a lad, his own religious temperament was not fully awakened. His old nurse and chief religious mentor used to encourage him to take refuge from his fears in the repetition of the name of the deity, Ramanama. Gandhi found this no help in his youth but the mature Gandhi, as well as the aged Mahatma, returned to this practice with gratitude. In his later trials and long fastings, he found the repetition of the name of a deity a source of strength.

Despite much opposition from his devout Hindu family, Gandhi pursued the suggestion of a family friend to go to England to study law that he might eventually follow in the footsteps of his deceased father. The devout mother only agreed when young Gandhi vowed to abstain from wine, women and meat during his absence. Though Gandhi was ordered by the Modh Bania caste **not** to proceed with his plans, he ignored their formal order and thus became an outcast in which status he remained even 'til the time of his death.

Though his vegetarian vow caused him difficulty in this strange land, he was determined to remain faithful. Gandhi tells that, at first, he was motivated in his vegetarian choice by health and economy. Religious motives held no prominent role in those early days. His biographer notes, however, that his "vegetarian by choice" status became an instrument of religion.

A pair of brothers whom Gandhi met in a vegetarian restaurant asked him to read *The Song Celestial,* the *Gita* with them. Shamefacedly, the young Gandhi had to confess that this was his first acquaintance with the poem. Upon reading it however, Gandhi found something extremely personal in it–something that was already deeply rooted within him. Another acquaintance, a good Christian, persuaded him to buy and read the Bible. Gandhi made little progress with the Old Testament but he was stirred to great excitement with the New, particularly with "The Sermon on the Mount."

When Gandhi completed his studies in England he sailed for India immediately. His shyness did him a great disservice as a barrister and his first attempts at law were nearly absolute failures. Gandhi therefore accepted a position in South Africa. There, after a year had passed, he undertook the cause of the Indian poor. His main interest was to help the indentured Indians gain self respect through teaching, self-discipline, truthfulness, cleanliness and overcoming dissention with the enemy.

M. GERMAINE HUSTEDDE, PHJC

During this time Gandhi never stopped his readings of various religions. One of the most decisively influential works of this time was Tolstoy's <u>The Kingdom of God is Within You</u>. Its effect was profound and remained with Gandhi until the end of his life. Interestingly, the theme of this book is that "The Sermon on the Mount" is a sufficient guide for one's life. Gandhi also pursued some of the later works of Tolstoy. *The Gospel in Brief* and *What to Do?* impressed Gandhi so much that he decided to write the author. A correspondence ensued between the two and Tolstoy recognized in Gandhi "the existence of a rare spirit, an element of the most undeniable greatness."[5]

At about the age of thirty-four Gandhi was approaching a decisive period in his life. The religious thought, the dietary reforms and sacrifice for others, which were his gifts by nature and temperament began to mature into a system. It was around this time that the <u>Gita</u> began to assume a place in his consciousness. He began memorizing the long poem in Sanskrit. Non-possession and non-attachment, the cardinal rule of the <u>Gita,</u> became the guide of Gandhi's life and he came to realize more and more, that the things which seemed like "great discoveries were always of things which already existed within him."[6]

Truth and Service

Consciously or unconsciously, Gandhi realized that he was being called in a special way. He realized, too, that poverty, chastity and humility must permeate the very being of anyone called to be a religious leader. The biographer notes that Gandhi's own nature brought him to this awareness and he vowed to live a life embracing these virtues. One of Gandhi's great gifts was his program of Satyagraha which derives its name from satya (truth) and agraha (firmness or a kind of force). He never swerved from these principles which informed his character.

Gandhi's political activity, though great, was only one aspect of his life. Though it changed the world and brought him to martyrdom, his biographer does not feel that the political aspect of Gandhi's career is the main element of significance. He believes that Gandhi's life was one vowed to martyrdom. His life was built upon the highest kind of service and in this he discovered his own depths.

The life of service allowed Gandhi's spirit to emerge. The self mastery required of him was great. He was called upon to renounce the egoistic possession of himself and he did not shrink from the cost.

Gandhi's call is seemingly different from the rank and file of humankind. Upon close examination we realize that this is not true. His call was essentially the same as ours—to come to the most perfect integration of body and spirit, to realize one's deepest self. It is true that the circumstances are different. We are not all called to be great champions of the poor, or to be directly instrumental in the cause of peace, but we are all called to the realization of our authentic selves though our loving involvement and concern for others.

The struggle which Gandhi waged in his own self-conquest is evident repeatedly throughout his biography. The discipline of non-possession left him with just the bare necessities of life. Everything that he might hold by way of trust (not possession) was to be used for the good of the poor. Gandhi's life was a blessed balance of possession and giving. He grew to an intimate sense of self-awareness and self-mastery. He often regretted that politics took so much of his time but he never permitted anything to interfere with his morning and evening prayers, the chanting of the hymns, his mediation and readings. Through discipline and intimate times of self encounter, he came to authentic self-possession. From this fullness, Gandhi was able to give, and it spilled over into every aspect of his life.

Through reflection and prayerful attentiveness, Gandhi put 'flesh' on the fundamental principles or theories that guided him. It was then, in this openness and commitment that the spirit overflowed in giving to others. It is the same for each of us. If I truly love, it cannot be stealthily locked within me. It overflows with a smile, sympathy, or compassion expressed in word or deed. Perhaps it takes the form of an act of kindness, or a donation for the poor and starving of our world. Whatever form it takes, it is death to self-love and ego-centeredness. This makes possible a new and deeper dimension of life–loosing oneself and embarking toward encounter with the Holy. It is the liberty that sets me free!

M. GERMAINE HUSTEDDE, PHJC

NOTES:

1. Cf. II Timothy, 3:1 ff.
2. Cf. Jean Moroux, The Meaning of Man, trans. A.H.G. Downes (New York: Sheed and Ward, 1952) p.131.
3. Moroux, Op. Cit., p.151.
4. Biographical data taken from Vincent Sheean, Lead Kindly Light (New York: Random House, 1949).
5. Sheean, Op. Cit., p.87.
6. Ibid., p 102.

THE CENTER

METANOIA GROUND

Is it the plan of God, to help me grow
To know . . . that

—unless a grain of wheat is sown
It remains alone;

—the mighty are cast down,
The lowly lifted up!

—that emptiness and nothingness
precede the brim-full cup?

I believe it is the plan of God
to teach my longing soul,
that through both darkness and the light
fragmentation is made whole.

I believe it is the way of God
To let me be cast down;
Then from God's reservoir of grace
Healing can be found.

Now with clear intensity
Is given me to know—
The many opposites of life,
With sacred space between
Is fruitful metanoia ground
Where paschal mystery abounds!

FOR REFLECTION:

What fragmentation in my life needs to be made whole.

What tension of the opposites have I experienced?

When have I experienced the paschal mystery in my life?

CHAPTER THIRTEEN

A SUFFICIENT GUIDE FOR ONE'S LIFE

UNTIL I AM wholly caught up in Christ, my pursuit of wholeness will remain incomplete. Striving toward wholeness is the task of the Christian and it is marked out for us in the Beatitudes[1] so that we can pursue that life-long call with a sufficient guide for the way. The Beatitudes, taken seriously, can be a guide for our entire lives. They can guide our choices, ignite our goals, and give hope and pursuit to our dreams. In a sense, the Beatitudes are the Commandments turned inside out.

The paradox that Christianity is, is manifested in the Beatitudes. Though the words are poetical, the song that emerges is somewhat dissonant to the egotistical, selfish and idealistic me. The Beatitudes seem contrary, contradictory, even revolutionary, as a way of self-emergence. They are, however, a pattern of fulfillment for the empty clay vessel that I am. They eminently provide a method of making room for God in my life.

The message perceived from this song demands a completely different response from the one I am accustomed to making. As I open myself and listen carefully, it becomes obvious that in each of the Beatitudes the Lord is speaking about a posture of the heart. This inner call is the important one to consider. False "be-attitudes" crumble in the face of the deeper message.

The Poor in Spirit

"Blessed are the poor in spirit, the Kingdom of heaven is theirs." How is it that we can skip over the words "in sprit" and almost immediately become fixated on the word "poor"? Poverty of spirit is meant to fashion an inner focus on God as the center of my life and guide me as a fundamental attitude. I skirt the call to 'poverty of spirit' when I fail to recognize that anything I may have by way of possession: materially, physically, mentally or even spiritually, is gift. My life is not my own! Of myself, I am nothing and have nothing. God is the Giver! God's chosen People knew and understood this. They were the *anawim*, God's poor.

Unless I am steeped in this sweeping awareness, my 'pot of gold' may take on varied forms such that I delude myself into believing that I live this basic call. Power, prestige, publicity, renown, etc., can fill the coffers of my heart and detour me from my goal, and at the same time leave the mansions of my spirit, my inner self, dry, desolate and distraught. Just as a healthy mind dwells in a healthy body, so, too does a healthy, happy spirit find its dwelling in a healthy, happy heart. It is a known fact that if I seek only my comfort, my gratification and my pleasure, I will only find myself.

The symbol of the empty nest may be a good one to reflect upon relative to "poverty of spirit". The empty nest speaks to me of detachment, openness and receptivity. If something is empty, it can be filled. Because I have little by way of material possessions it does not mean that I am detached, or poor in the Beatitude sense of things. Living in too much daily comfort and security can vitiate, also, against genuine poverty of spirit. Only when I have emptied my life of superfluous "riches" like clinging to my opinions, basking in my comfort and plenty, clutching insignificant items and climbing the mountain of 'Acclaim' can my nest, my sprit, be filled with God who alone can satisfy all my desires. Only in the light of His love, His magnanimous generosity and all-embracing goodness, can I begin to understand what "poverty of spirit" really means.

Many people throughout the world know existentially, what a curse material and physical poverty can be. Parents have watched their children waste away for lack of food and die miserable deaths. They stand by helplessly—suffering one of the greatest poverties: the inability to help those in need. Homeless children spend their days foraging for scarps of food and often being sleepless at night. One of the Street boys recently wrote to me, "Pray for me because I want God to give me a heart like yours.

You saved me! I used to sleep under donkey carts at night, but when it was raining, for many nights I could not sleep at all."

The spiritual poverty to which Christ invites us is safeguarded by the invitation I receive from time to time, to curb my inordinate desires for more. It seems our society is ever looking for more pleasure, relaxation, more bodily comfort. In the light of our brothers and sisters of the developing and under-developed countries, and even suffering neighbors in this continent, we are certainly called to a life of moderation. How can I do with less in order that others may have more or even their rightful share?

Poverty of spirit is a matter of the heart. Having a concern for others is surely a vestige of poverty of spirit! God's love for me is no more or less than that which HE has for the poorest of human kind. When I open the door of my heart to others I am receptive of God's love as well as being God's messenger.

The Meek

"Blessed are the meek, they shall inherit the land." In our culture, meekness is often considered the stance of the weak. For some it connotes undue submissiveness or a 'milk-toasty' personality. A meek person is then assumed to be a coward. On the other hand, how sure we must all be that violence and terrorism are not acceptable modes of response in any provocation. Each of us needs to cultivate a mode of tolerance and acceptance that is the foundation of the virtue of meekness.

The ideal of meekness is portrayed in Christ's own life and it seems to embody His statement "Learn of Me for I am meek and humble of heart." A meek person is patient under provocation. Contemporary culture clamors for self-assertion, retaliation, revenge. Our world today is full of violence and boisterous conduct. On the other hand, meekness portrays gentleness. Meekness is opposed to selfish, personal fulfillment. The truly meek person has a capacity to transcend hurts and slights, the negative opinion of others, and even false judgments, to grow in disciplined love.

A meek person is one who is accessible. Meekness bears the quality of being able to affirm others; to forgive! Think of the stature of a man like

Christ who was equally at home with the saint and the sinner. Perhaps the greatest act of Christ's meekness was that of forgiving His executioners from the altar of the Cross. "Father, forgive them; they do not know what they are doing." [2]

Many examples have come down to us through the experiences of our Jewish brothers and sisters who were so maligned during the Holocaust, as well as stalwart men and women who openly resisted this evil on their behalf. One of these great personages, a survivor, is Elie Wiesel, the Nobel Peace Prize winner of 1986. He shows us the depth of forgiveness. He recounts horrendous experiences of watching men, women and children gassed and thrown into open graves. He agonized with his dying father, saw him mistreated and maligned. Even in his last hours he was unable to help him. The magnitude of Elie's heart and that of other survivors is that they nurtured no spirit of revenge. When they finally were set free, it was a freedom both of body and spirit.

Throughout life it may happen that I have been slighted, by-passed, unnoticed, and perhaps even on some rare occasion, accused falsely. My response to these slights bespeaks the extent of my meekness. Do I complain? Do I nurse grudges? Do I grow cranky and bitter in disposition? Do I forgive? Not to do so is to betray the God who is LOVE.

The objective, inherent truth in meekness seems to be the ability to be joyful. We are the only ones of God's creation who have the ability to respond in joy to the gift of life. Do I attempt to be a joyful presence? Can I suffer rebuff and seeming disregard, or grave disappointment without giving way to morose, bitter feelings? Can I be wronged, intentionally or unintentionally, and still be joyful? Can I abandon myself into God's hands and trust that "All will be well"? [3]

Perhaps another small interjection is of value. The meek shall inherit 'the land' Scripture says. Does this beatitude perhaps call us likewise to reflect upon our attitude toward the 'earth' we hope to inherit or leave for posterity? What is my attitude toward this beautiful planet on which I live? Am I Ok with exploitation, unjust distribution of its resources, insensitivity to waste and overconsumption? Just as my life is not my own—so too, the planet earth belongs to the whole of humankind. It is only given to us in trust by our loving God.

Blessed, Those Who Mourn

Our Lord promised that "those who mourn shall be comforted." What can this Beatitude possibly have to do with being a sure path for my life? Does it seem a bit far-fetched to you?

Consider for a moment how our human nature is heir to thousands of afflictions. In the natural order there is pain, bodily discomfort of all kinds, suffering, mental anxiety, the acute sense of loss at the death of a parent, spouse or loved one, rejection by a friend . . . ad infinitum. One cannot pick up a daily newspaper without becoming aware of our world as a "vale of tears". Discontent, inequity, joblessness, inflation, violence and death stare out at us from every page. Even the most fortunate of us cannot escape life without some sorrow.

In an even more deeply personal dimension there is the realization, at the very core of my being, that I am a wounded Individual, in need of healing. There is personal sin in my life which wounds and scars me. It often produces gross unrest. I fail again and again, and am often laden with anxiety and guilt. But this very awareness should trigger too, the awareness that God's merciful love far exceeds any sense of guilt I may have. Wallowing in guilt is the exact opposite of spiritual mourning. God knows my weakness, my human frailty. Owning this reality and facing up to it opens the door of my heart to God's encompassing embrace! God does not love me in spite of my weakness, but because of it! When I enlarge my understanding of what it means to mourn I begin to welcome the wisdom of God who teaches me that where I am in my own process of becoming, is where God will meet me and it is there that I will meet God.

Spiritual mourning does not exclude sorrow in the natural order. Rather it sanctifies it. We are motivated to place our trust in the redemptive mystery and turn to Christ "who never fails to comfort those who are brought low."4 If my mourning leads to doom and dejection, it is not the mourning proclaimed by Christ in the Beatitudes. Keen mental perception enables me to see beyond the momentary sorrow and possible daily loss. Just yesterday someone shared the poignant story of a mother who had been an invalid for many years. Finally, the dear mother passed away. The son, who bore his mother's handicap and incapacity, through all the years he cared for her was now able to say at the graveside, "Now, mother is set free!" This person could see beyond his present loss and rejoice with the new found freedom of his own dear mother.

Any mature person knows that suffering, pain and death are inescapable realities of life. Personal sorrow ought to sharpen my sense of sympathy and responsibility for another, perhaps making me "feel" for the other in a unique way. Jesus wept over Jerusalem. He felt the death of Lazarus, his friend, like all humans experience such loss. He was not afraid to let his emotions be seen. There is an old Indian proverb that says, "Unless there is a tear in your eye, there cannot be a rainbow in your heart." The Greek word "kara" means to lament or cry out. It is also the entomology of our English word *care*. When have I reached out to someone, possibly cried with someone over a loss or misfortune to let them know that I really care? Sometimes it takes two to let that rainbow happen!

How blessed (fortunate) am I? Do I reflect Christ the Consoler to the suffering persons I meet on life's way? Do I put people above things and project an authentic concern about the needy of the world which I translate somehow into action? Gandhi was especially gifted in the ability to mourn with, and for, his people. The symbol of the spinning-wheel looms large in his ability to mourn. For Gandhi and for the people, the spinning-wheel was something beyond economics, politics or sociology. It was a kind of mystical emphasis upon service and 'feeling with' the poor. He translated that into action by seeking to improve the economic conditions of his country through the art of weaving. In Gandhi's mature life, he devoted four hours each day to spinning. In this, Gandhi felt drawn to the poorest of the poor and in them to the Divine.[5]

Hunger and Thirst . . .

"Blessed are those who hunger and thirst for righteousness; they shall be satisfied." Some translations speak of hungering and thirsting for holiness. Is there a great difference?

"The word Matthew uses in urging us to seek first God's way of holiness is *dikaiosyne*, or righteousness (justice). . . . To achieve the constitutive experience of God's justice in us, we are to hunger and thirst for God's life, saving power and care for us."[6] When God's life in us has reached perfection we are justified and have attained holiness. Justice, in the Scriptural sense can also be translated as right living.

When God brought back the Israelites from the land of exile, God empowered Moses to bring forth water from the rock to satisfy their thirst. God also supplied manna from heaven as sustenance for the weary travelers. Like of old, we are a journeying people in whom the ancient Exodus is daily repeated. We move from one plane of life, to another, seeking and searching for true Christian fulfillment and liberty. Deep in our hearts we know that we can never be satisfied. Of necessity, we strain toward the infinite. The hunger and thirst at the very center of our human existence is our radical tendency toward the all loving God. Authentic spiritual hunger and thirst become an ardent longing to do what God desires of us. This calls me to creative fidelity. van Croonenburg expresses this movement somewhat like this. Human life will always be subject to the ever-changing situations in which we find ourselves and 'communion with the Absolute Thou' is no different. Therefore the price on our part is that of 'continuous struggle and absolute fidelity'. This is what enables us to bear the insecurity and obscurity of our journey and eventually come to the end point 'where we will experience the presence of True Love.'[7]

We may achieve a momentary sense of fulfillment, but human nature, being what it is, can never succeed in remaining at this height. In the ups and downs that ensue, we may come to discouragement. We may even experience a mistrust similar to that which prompted Moses to strike the rock twice, instead of complying with God's specific command. In the natural order, we hunger and thirst because we long to live. In the spiritual order we hunger and thirst more and more to be united with our God.

The person who hungers and thirsts after justice, grows in communion. Only Christ can fill one's life. Christ becomes the food and drink that can sustain and satisfy us in the journey of life. Since the Holy Other is the ONE for whom we thirst and hunger, we may well substitute the word "holiness" for justice. Paul tells us in letter to the Romans that "God loves us and calls us to be holy."[8]

In the Thirteenth Showing of Julian of Norwich, we are instructed that the longing we have for our God is God's hunger and thirst for us.

> *As truly as there is in God a property of compassion and pity, so truly is there in Him a property of thirst and longing. By virtue of this longing in Christ, we have to long for him in response. Without this response, no soul comes to heaven. The property of hunger and thirst comes from the endless goodness of God.*[9]

The Gospel story of the 'Woman at the Well'[10] portrays of one of the most sincere seekers. The woman, looking for water that would quench bodily thirst, was rewarded with Christ own gift of Himself. She allowed the 'breaking Light' to quench her deepest desire. "Lord, give me always this water!" Truly, it was the endless goodness of God that brought her to this particular time and space. In this very first encounter, she witnessed a radical conversion in herself and became one of Jesus' disciples. This is what true hunger and thirst must do for each of us and it is the acid test of our sincerity and commitment.

We cannot receive what we do not intensely desire. Through prayer and meditation we are drawn more deeply into an encounter with Christ. Each meeting serves to draw us to another. We begin to relish moments of stillness, prayer and nearness to our God. These precious moments are an oasis in our earthly desert experience and they are also the magnet that draws us to hunger and thirst for more!

M. GERMAINE HUSTEDDE, PHJC

Blessed—the Merciful

When we consider the Beatitude, "Blessed are the merciful for they shall obtain mercy," we are brought up short with the need we ourselves have for divine mercy. When I recognize myself as 'sinner', I cannot escape this reality. This realization results not from a haphazard effort "to be good" but from the continued and determined striving of a person, in a unique and individual way, to draw near to God.

As we grow and strive for maturation in the natural order, we realize that we violate some of the norms for perfect health and mental vigor. We indulge in just a few more snacks, one more cookie or some 'junk food' which we do not need at all. Sometimes we become like couch potatoes, glued for hours to TV transmissions that definitely have no value for mental acumen or social awareness. We honor our wants more than our needs!

Growth in Christ demands adherence to the Commandments, but again and again I find myself transgressing and falling short of God's expectations. In the Sermon on the Mount, our Lord mapped out the Christian life of perfection thus exposing us again to the Decalogue in a very positive and rewarding way. The Beatitudes say nothing about sin and yet they are addressed to sinners.

The virtue of mercy is characteristic of God. It is not natural to human beings. We only begin to understand genuine mercy when we keep our eyes fixed on Christ in the Gospels. The Prodigal Son, the thief crucified with Christ, the woman accused of adultery and the Magdalene, each was a recipient of the mercy of Christ. Christ tells them that He came to save sinners. Each of these penitents acknowledged themselves as such, and each was rewarded with God's embracing love.

The awareness of personal sin and my need of redemption prompt me to rely on the same mercy which Christ so lovingly portrayed in the Gospels. Realizing that I, too, am one of the sick in need of the ministrations of the Divine Physician, prayer wells up from my heart: "Have mercy on me a sinner." The author of <u>Living Prayer,</u> noted that the modern translation of the words "have mercy" is too weak and insufficient to impart the deep significance implied. The Greek word <u>*eleison*</u> which we translate as "have mercy" has the same root as _elaion_ which designates olive trees and the oil taken from them.[11]

Throughout the Old Testament we find the symbol of the olive tree connoting peace. For example in the book of Genesis we read the familiar account of Noah, how he released the dove and it returned with the olive branch of peace. Oil was used for the anointing of Kings. In the New Testament oil is used to heal the Samaritan who fell among the robbers. Summarizing the healing power of oil, Bloom says that oil connotes first of all 'the end of the wrath of God'. In the symbol of the olive branch God was offering peace to the people who had offended him. He goes on to say that oil speaks of God's healing that we might live authentically and 'become what [God] has called us to be' [12]

But it does not end there! I am admonished to show concern, care and compassion in the same measure as I have received it. Intolerance, prejudice or lack of forgiveness on my part sets up barriers to my own personal reception of God's mercy. Because God has shown mercy to us it demands that we be merciful to one another. Perhaps it requires me to cultivate a lively sensitivity to the needs of others, to rout any vestige of favoritism from my life, to stand up for those who are alienated in society, for any form of injustice. Exclusiveness or margination of any kind vitiates against the true quality of mercy.

Even a cursory reflection upon the limitless mercy of Christ should call upon all of us to stand staunchly against the horrors of Capital Punishment. Who are we to take justice into our own hands when this is clearly the right and prerogative of a loving God? We all have a stake in every execution. Each time someone is to be executed the report states "N.N. is scheduled to be executed by the people of Texas", for example. It sends shivers into my whole being and is very repulsive to me. God's mercy can never be exhausted and each of us could probably say, "There go I, except for the grace and mercy of my God." On Robert Kennedy's tombstone in Arlington cemetery are carved the words " . . . Each time a man stands up for an ideal or acts to improve the lot of others or strikes against injustice he sends forth a tiny ripple of hope; and crossing each other from a million centers of energy and daring, these ripples build a current that can sweep down

M. GERMAINE HUSTEDDE, PHJC

the mightiest walls of oppression and resistance." Can we be that current that can 'sweep down" the resistance to do away with Capital Punishment throughout the entire United States?

Another example: I remember the struggle that ensued when I approached the Head Teacher to enroll the Street Boys we were caring for in Kenya, in the parochial school system. While the Head Teacher himself was open and sympathetic to the request, the teachers were resistant and very negative. Their combined attitude was that the Boys would be a bad example to the other pupils and that the median scores would suffer because these boys were literally unschooled and initially rather undisciplined. To me, it was understandable. They had lived for years on the Street, fending for themselves, having no schedule, no responsibility except to keep body and soul alive. It was their daily task and struggle. Some were already in their teens and had never had the opportunity to sit in a classroom for a single day. The teachers relented on their prejudice after I approached the District Education Officer and explained the situation to him. I requested that the Boys be given a trial of one semester to prove themselves in the established system, without having to include their scores along with the other pupils. The DEO readily agreed, so the matter was more or less settled, at least for three months–the duration of a semester. I met with the Boys and impressed upon them how important it would be for their future to behave well and be disciplined in their new educational endeavor. The Boys did not disappoint me! No one could take issue with their behavior and they took to their books and lessons with avid interest. I have never seen kids so highly motivated! At the end of the Semester they achieved the rank of first, second or third in their class. The teachers' theory no longer supported them and they were forced to manifest some 'compassion'.

Modern day stories of mercy abound. Read "The Miracle at Tenwek" (by Gregg Lewis) and be awed by the compassion and servant hood of Dr. Ernie Steury, a native of Auburn, Indiana. It is a compelling story of one man's love for the poor and sick and the ripple effect his compassion had in a small Kenyan village, outside of Bomet.

One experience I had in our small Kenyan village has etched itself into my memory such that it can never be erased. It is the opposite of the mercy and compassion which Dr. Stuery displays. One morning we were on the way to the village church for morning Eucharist. Already from a distance, one could observe a large gathering of people close by a little settlement. They were not rowdy, loud or boisterous, but stood around quite calmly, so initially, we were not alarmed. As we neared, we observed a body of a young man—probably no more than a youth, lying in the middle of the road. Evidence and cause of his death were still quite visible. The scorched area encircling his tortured body shocked us all. Here was a young man whom the 'people' decided was a thief. A rubber tire had been placed over his head and around his neck. Then it was doused with kerosene and set afire. The young man burned to death. His lifeless body lie there convicting humankind of its lack of mercy! I could never pass that way again without praying for the young man and his executioners.

Mercy helps me to experience all people as members of the family of Christ, each of whom has been redeemed by His Precious Blood. I cannot pick and choose those deserving of love. I am not a judge! Mercy, if it is to be like Christ's, admits of no selectivity, no favoritism and no judgment on my part.

Purity of Heart

"Blessed are the pure of heart for they shall see God"!

While Scripture scholars seem not to have come to an exhaustive interpretation of this beatitude, I believe the emphasis must be placed on the word "heart"—an interior disposition. This requires the full oblation of every single-minded person. Throughout life we are prevailed upon to modify our hierarchy of values. We learn to relinquish a great many things which we had categorized as absolute necessity, expedient or perhaps merely satisfying. As life gradually unfolds, we find that the things we held in such high esteem smack of superfluity or even bitterness. Nothing comes completely up to my expectations.

It is through 'purity of heart' that we seek, and eventually come to "see" the face of God. Truly, no one of this earth has even really seen God—but like the Psalmist we 'lift our eyes to the mountain'. You will recall that Jesus beheld God, the Father, on Mt. Tabor, the mount of the Transfiguration.[13] What the Apostles saw in His marvelously transfigured appearance was His purity of heart, an openness and transparency which embodied His presence with God. This manifested itself as bright as the noon-day sun. Again Kierkegaard reminds us that "Purity of heart is to will one thing . . ."[14] For Christ, 'the one thing' was the will of the Father and in Him the Father was well pleased.

For the pure of heart, life is well integrated. There is a radical constancy which reaches deep into the person's life, allowing ones' self to be drawn straight forward to intense spiritual living and a child-like awareness of God's love for me. It is not only 'awareness'; it often goes deeper than that! It is more like being 'at home' with God. The pure of heart can meet God everywhere: in nature, a flower, a child. It is an innate awareness that I must re-discover.

Ages ago, when I was assigned to care of pre-school children in St. Vincent's Home in Ft. Wayne, Indiana, I was often amused and awed by the children's intrinsic sense of goodness and purity of heart. Because we were low in funds and consequently short of hired help, the Girls, who were already in Secondary School, but resident in the Home, assisted with bathing, dressing and grooming of the 'Nursery Kids'. You can imagine that some thirty plus small children each awaiting their turn, often found ways to entertain themselves. One day, Kathy, a truly beautiful child, repeatedly got in the way of one of the older girls who was working, against time, to complete her tasks before she would leave for school. Kathy would stand at the mirror and admire her long blond hair, reach for the comb of the older girls and primp away to her heart's content. Several times the aid politely asked Kathy to sit down and wait her turn, but little Kathy persisted in making a nuisance of herself. Finally, exasperated, the aid said rather sharply to Kathy, "Kathy, SIT down! You're ugly anyway!" I was shocked and about to remonstrate when Kathy smiled, pulled herself up tall and said "No I'm not! God made me!!"

I mused on how one so young and so composed, could be so sure of herself in relationship to her God. She recognized innately, God's love for her through her very existence. Kathy's wisdom passed far beyond the surface of things to the level of the heart.

The pure of heart are drawn to God as moths to a flame! For the pure of heart there is a gradual sloughing off of everything in life that is superfluous or trifling in favor of the compelling desire to be only with and for God.

We know the old adage, "The eye is the mirror of the soul." Recently, I was called to reflect further upon a similar aphorism which chided, "The eyes search for that for which the heart longs"!

I am sure you have met someone whose eyes seemed to be so clear and piercing that they looked into the depths of your very self. This was my experience as I was privileged to have a private audience with the Holy Father, Pope Paul VI. His gaze was so intent and clear, I thought he could read my soul. In relationship to purity of heart, the "eyes' have it! The focus of my eye on God does not detract from my consideration of others. In fact, it enhances it! It orders me to live in a caring posture toward everyone. My considerations and dealings with others direct me toward the broader horizon of my life—God's love for me and for all of Creation. Living thus approximates single-mindedness . . . the desire to embrace the will of God totally and to live in gratitude for each and every blessing.

Sometimes, it is difficult for us to recognize a blessing because we have not learned to be sufficiently detached. Detachment is comparable to a small death, a dying to self and it is far from easy! Surely all that transpires in life is not agreeable to me. I may prefer a certain ministry, a definite location. I may go to lengths to explain why this particular apostolate, in this particular place, is 'best' for me. I am convinced that all my reasons for submitting the request to those in authority are legitimate and worthy of consideration. Then comes the 'axe'! The administration decides that it is best that my request is answered in the negative. It is part of our daily dying. Paul Tillich catches this truth beautifully when he says that everyday a little of our life is taken from us. He concludes that since every day we die a little the final hour of our passing 'merely completes the process.'[15]

If in my daily round of events, I may be influenced to see beyond the subjective horizon of selfish pride and egoistic self-fulfillment to something beyond my arbitrary will and pleasure, I may be graced to grow in purity of heart. This is truly God's desire for me! With God's grace I may develop a spiritual vision which enables me to discern deeper values and to appreciate the mystery bound up with all of life even though I cannot understand it fully. What really matters is my *way* of service, not *where* I am assigned but the *how* which is the expression of my love. A new orientation predominates as I grow in single-mindedness.

The person who is pure of heart is protected from the undue power of fad and fashion. One is able to pierce the myth of the fashionable and modern and weigh implicitly, the values acclaimed by the crowd. Certain meaningful activities and observances, regarded by others as outmoded and useless, are held in reverence and respect. The pure of heart perceive true and inherent values. Instead of life becoming more complicated with the passage of time and years, it becomes more simple. Simplicity is the guardian of purity of heart.

Purity of heart is the environment needed to see the path that God has laid out for me. It is the price and reward of intimate union with the Beloved. When the nest of my heart is cluttered, harboring vain and useless desires, I am not free enough to follow the path that will guide me into the loving arms of my God. The baggage I carry weighs me down and I am not able to make the leap that propels me into God's loving embrace.

In summary we could say that this Beatitude is all about growing in, and living in, God's Presence until we are so united with our God that we are 'oned' with Him.

Blessed are the Peacemakers

Recently I participated in an icon painting Retreat advertised as "A Brush with God". Because I had to cancel the retreat for which I was previously scheduled, I resorted to this one, primarily to fulfill an obligation. But I had a certain feeling of apprehension. I did not consider myself an artist, by any means, and I thought of the fiasco for which I was setting myself up. In the very first encounter with the Director, he allayed most of my fears. Very gently, but emphatically, he remarked that 'this retreat is about the process; *not* about the product.'

I feel quite certain that we must look at being peacemakers in quite the same way. Indeed, we all want peace, in ourselves, in families, in communities, in our world. This is the product we long for! But the process is all important!!

Scripture shows something of God's plan for peace. Ever attuned to the will of the Father, Jesus sought to rearrange the existing order of things. The lowly would be exalted; the high and mighty would be dethroned and the poor would have the gospel preached to them. Jesus chose humble fishermen to be His emissaries and companions. Learning from the example of Jesus it is obvious that peace follows justice.

Peace is a gift which is based on right relationships. Jesus' relationship with God was that of Son to Father. The sure and lasting bond was proclaimed at Jesus' Baptism and ratified again on the Mount of the Transfiguration: "This is my Son, the Beloved; with him I am well pleased."[16]

As persons, and as a society, we can disregard the process which leads to peace and commiserate the reality of war, violence and bloodshed. We fail to notice that the right relationship between ourselves and God has been disturbed as well as our commitment among the people of our family, our community and our world. No peace can exist where injustice, inequity in the distribution of the world's resources, bias, prejudice and unfair practices dominate. The road to peace necessarily passes through the way of justice. Though we cannot solve these problems in the space allotted here, we need to be called to a renewed awareness of our responsibility to the cause of justice and peace.

Allow me to resort to an example once again. Gandhi espoused the cause of peace in his life. Having dedicated himself to the cause of truth (Satyagraha) he insisted that both sides of any dispute be addressed with attentive love, and that one must never take unfair advantage of another. Gandhi insisted that under all conditions, even under violence, that non-violence was to prevail. The Salt March or Gandhi's March to the Sea ended at Port Dandi. It was a pilgrimage which the whole world watched. Immense crowds followed Gandhi from village to village. At the sea Gandhi made a "handful of salt out of the sea-water–a symbol instantly understood in all languages; the foreign government claimed a monopoly on salt which was God's gift to everybody . . ."[17] Gandhi was subsequently imprisoned. Paradoxically, Gandhi's espousal to peace was the cause of his violent death, but his death led to peace. Gandhi was not only wedded to peace but to the example of Christ that he found in the Scriptures.

True peace is not a superficial gift. It floods the whole self with blessed freedom. The initial salutation, "Peace be with you!" of a kindly confessor impresses me every time I am greeted with it as I approach the sacrament of Reconciliation. This is a sacrament which embodies a movement toward internal, personal peace. I realize as I acknowledge my sins to God's representative that the source of my greatest unrest arises from my pride and selfishness, my lack of love and justice. True peace is effected in my life only when I am able to move from self-centeredness and staunch egoism to embrace the designs and laws of a loving and merciful God. The peace or non-peace which my life may embody spills over to those with whom I come in contact also.

My act of faith in Christ's embracing and merciful forgiveness is supplemented by His response. The peace I experience is the strong bond of the Father's love which renews me in the status of son/daughter-ship.

Peace negates agitation and restlessness. It casts out fear. Fear for each of us may take myriad forms. With the extremely poor, the fear of not having sufficient food, clothing, shelter, is always very real. It shows itself in a tendency to be greedy when food is available, to be overly protective of what one has, to be wary of losing one's 'shelter' even if it consists merely of a large carton. I have seen this scenario played out repeatedly in the life of the Street Children. Their lives are so insecure in every way. But I have also seen them change into sharing, caring and loving individuals once their basic needs are met. The tendencies to be greedy, quarrelsome and aggressive give way to efforts to integrate them into a 'family', a loving community. The plight of the poor cannot be disregarded if we are in earnest about peace. It is a moral obligation to right the wrongs they experience. Justice must be the handmaid of peace!

The temptation to forget about God's providential care will claim no hold on me if I have attempted to cultivate an attitude of trust. At the same time, I will not be so callous as to think that it is God's task alone to bring peace to our warring world. The "be-attitude" of peace which engages me in the service of peacemaking is built of the serene and quiet acceptance of the happenings of my daily life. This inner calm points to a beautiful harmony between God and the soul. It reflects the peace and presence of His love to those with whom I come in contact.

I ought to reflect upon myself as an instrument of peace. Can I find meaning in the difficult and hard things of life? Am I able to look beyond the external trappings and trust in the providential care of the all-loving God? If I can trust in God's love despite the dire circumstances around me, I can be at peace.

Peace-making is a corporate venture. No one goes the way alone. Peace and lack of peace are both 'infectious'. If I am not at peace, I will spread unrest and agitation. We observe this graphically in the hundreds and thousands who join in protest marches. But the opposite is also true. There have been peace rallies in the cause of justice that have had remarkable results. We need but think of personages such as Rosa Parks, Martin Luther King or Sojourner Truth. As the well-known song has it, peace must begin with me.

Our world today desperately needs to renew the sentiments of St. Francis' prayer: Lord, make me an instrument of peace. How? Where there is hatred, let me sow love. Where there is injury—pardon!

We all need to be staunch supporters of the movements toward peace. Every act of violence, aggression, animosity and hatred tears at the seamless robe of Christ. We are all one body, one world, one universe! When we destroy one another in fits of retaliation, war and destruction, we destroy ourselves, too.

It was Martin Luther King's dream and hope that one day peace would reign. In his acceptance speech of the Nobel Peace Prize in 1968 he summed up his hope thus: "I believe that one day, man shall bow down before the altars of God and be crowned triumphant over war and bloodshed, and nonviolent goodwill will proclaim the rule of the land."

For this dream to come true, every person must engage him/herself with a fully committed determination. We must believe that it is not only Martin Luther King's dream but also God's wish!

M. GERMAINE HUSTEDDE, PHJC

Blessed those who suffer persecution in the cause of justice . . .

Thomas More, the learned but simple, Lord Chancellor of England seems to be an embodiment of this beatitude. One who is persecuted is usually harassed and oppressed because of some exemplary witness to the cause of Christ or perhaps because of staunch fidelity to an ideal. Thomas More was no exception. More's high regard for marriage, for family life, for justice and honesty were intrinsic values that he regarded so highly that he irritated those of lesser moral standards. Even when King Henry VIII's will dominated most of the Kingdom, More's adherence to his noble philosophy prevailed. Compromise was beneath Thomas.

Having refused to take the oath which acknowledged Henry as the Supreme Head of the Church of England, More fell into great disfavor with the King. During this time when trouble was brewing for him, Thomas, though outwardly professing a lightheartedness, later confided to his daughter, Margaret, the many anxiety filled and sleepless hours which burdened him with a heavy heart. More's family thought he was deliberately courting death. It grieved him to see his family suffer. The subsequent imprisonment of Thomas in the Tower of London, followed eventually by his execution, confirmed the family's dreaded fears. More faced his death with the usual philosophy that permeated his life. "Supposing, I lose my head" Thomas mused, "to the greater glory of his soul's journey, no one could come headless for 'our head is Christ' and therefore to him we must be joined . . ."[18] More was not spared the King's wrath, but he was preserved from the pang of a guilty conscience. More died affirming that he was "the King's good servant but God's first."[19]

Thomas More's example proclaims that persecution consists in a readiness to suffer for the sake of Christ. This disposition brought More to the necessity of making a fundamental choice between God and the King. It was, in reality, a choice that Thomas had practiced throughout his life. Thomas was so well-versed in the art of 'losing his life' that he could face his executioner's cheerfully.

Christians are bound to suffer because they stand in the world as a symbol of Christ. The Christian represents values of truth, justice and uprightness which are largely spurned by society. The Christian is often forced to stand alone. He is the paradoxical personage described by St. Paul:

We are treated as imposter, and yet are true;
As unknown, and yet well known;
Dying, and see—we are alive;
As punished and yet not killed;
Sorrowful, yet always rejoicing
Poor, yet making many rich;
As having nothing, yet possessing everything.[21]

The Beatitudes call for a renewed Gospel spirituality. Love and suffering are the two poles by which the Christian follows Christ. They are also the dialectic though which we advance to self-actualization. We could look upon love and suffering as the vertical and horizontal beams of the cross of life. They converge to form a mysterious affinity with Christ, the Exemplar of every life.

Conclusion

Taken singly or collectively, the Beatitudes show us that the way of life is happy and blessed for those of good will. Each trial of life becomes a way of greater love through which we can come to a more intense communion with Him who loved us first. Armed with a positive attitude, I answer the call to grow in Christ. With his grace it is possible to transfigure my limitations, trials, sufferings and persecutions. The path we follow is clear. It is the way of the Cross, but it is also the path of love, of blessedness—of happiness. It is in this close imitation of Christ that we find that God comes in to dwell with us.

The Beatitudes show us a pathway which Susan Muto develops extensively.[21] Through the threefold path of the deepening and living out of our faith, we are called to a new discipline, the purgative way. The Beatitudes, lived with commitment and fidelity can very definitely be a pattern of discipline through which we pass to a more intense understanding and acceptance of the role these norms must play in our lives. They lead us to a new light: the Light of Christ. Mystics call this the illuminative way which is the threshold to an intimate companionship with the Beloved. This results in the plane of union or in the culmination of the Unitive Way. This pattern or guide can surely be relied upon in our life's journey toward maturity and wholeness in Christ.

A great deal of unhappiness and misery in the world exists because of our inadequate and warped value system. Pleasure, power and acclaim may suffice for a while, but the tensions of life reduce these passing achievements to dross in the full glare of life. Intense and authentic living requires supernatural motivation. The beams of the cross stretch out to the four corners of the earth. They signify the extent of Christ's redeeming love and also remind us that the Christian must be concerned about our brothers and sisters throughout the world. Each of the Beatitudes breaks the confining bonds of self-love and narrow individualism and relates me in a broader spiritual dimension to God and humankind. How blest we are when the Beatitudes become the compass for our daily lives. We gradually live into the truth that the Beatitudes ARE a sufficient guide for our lives!

NOTES:

1. Cf. Matthew 5, 1-16
2. Luke 23: 34
3. Words spoken to Julian of Norwich. Cf. M.L.del Mastro, trans. <u>The Revelation of Divine Love in Sixteen Showings</u> (Triumph Books, Liguori. MO, 1977) p 108.
4. I Cor. 7:6.
5. Cf. Sheean, <u>Lead Kindly Light</u>., p.158.
6. Michael H Crosby, O.F.M. Cap., <u>Spirituality of the Beatitudes</u>, (Maryknoll, N.Y.: Orbis Books, 1981), p.121.
7. Cf. Van Croonenurg, <u>Gateway to Reality</u>. P. 128.
8. Romans 1: 7.
9. M.L. del Mastro. <u>Op. Cit</u>., p.107
10. Cf. Jn. 4
11. Anthony Bloom, <u>Living Prayer</u> (Springfield, IL., Templegate Publishers, 1966), pp. 86-87.
12. <u>Ibid.</u>
13. LK. 9: 2-36
14. Bradley Dewey, <u>The New Obedience,</u> p. 142.
15. Paul Tillich, <u>The Courage to Be</u> (New Haven, Conn.: Yale University Press, 1952) p.9.
16. Mt. 3: 17 & 17: 15
17. Sheean. <u>Lead Kindly Light</u>, p. 158.
18. Farrow, John. <u>The Story of Thomas More</u>. (New York: Sheed and Ward, 1954.) p.224.
19. <u>Ibid</u>., p.227
20. II Cor. 6:-10
21. Cf. Muto, Susan. <u>Blessings that Make us Be. A Formative Approach to Living the Beatitudes</u>, (Pittsburg, PA: Epiphany Books, 2001).

MANY GIFTS—ONE SPIRIT

COMPASSION

C entered, quiet and still,
O verflowing with peace. I open
M y mind and heart to
P eople—suffering ones, the needy
A nd cast-asides; those who long for the
S urety that comes with knowing that God cares and that
S ociety wllingingly reaches deep down into the
I NCARNATON MYSTERY—attuned to God, in His
"O ffice to save us—His glory to do it!"
N ever separating compassion from contemplation.

(Inspired by Showings. Pp. 300-302)

FOR REFLECTION:

What relationship do I find between compassion and contemplation?

What shows me that society is sufficiently willing to reach deep down into the Incarnation Mystery?

How can I assist the poor to come to the realization that "God cares"?

CHAPTER FOURTEEN

THE MOUNTAIN OF DECISION

IN THE MOST radical sense, spiritual growth and fulfillment is the only lasting and worthwhile accomplishment. Bodily satisfaction and ego achievements are momentarily satisfying, comparable to gossamer threads, filmy and ethereal which easily float away.

The fulfillment for which I yearn takes place in the deepest dimension of the self. It requires my effort, desire and determination, but it is God, more than myself, who works in me and graces all my efforts. My task is to keep myself in readiness for the moment when God sees fit to work His designs in me. God knows how weak and frail my strength is, but His love far exceeds my greatest weakness. Somewhere, St. Augustine has said that the greatest perfection of the individual is to discover one's imperfection. For me, this does not only mean sin, but my weakness and frailty; my utter dependence on the loving God. It is like allowing myself to be drenched in God's love—to soak it up like a sponge and to be fully inundated to the very core of my being.

In this task, God requires our fullest possible commitment. God will not tolerate half-heartedness. The visions of St. John in Revelations tell us that God loathes those who are neither "hot nor cold".[1] Half measures will not suffice! Full commitment is like an on-going liturgy in which God makes a covenant with us. God's love is constant, unchanging and unquestionable. My finiteness requires an on-going and oft-repeated response. Paul Hinnebusch expresses this concept saying that a person cannot commit the entire self (i.e. one's entire life) in one graced moment. The reason is that, except for this very moment, my "life" does not yet exist. It is 'future' because we do not live our lives all at once. Our life unfolds moment by moment and therefore I cannot give my entire life except by making a contract of it—giving it moment by moment as it comes into existence. As such, I will be fulfilling the promise as a 'ceaseless activity until the end of life'.[2]

God's covenant with us is His promise to sustain us. Jesus ratified God's covenant through His death on Calvary but to make a covenant fruitful and able to be fully accomplished, each of us must do our part. It is as though I must return to the mountain of decision every day, and many times each day as my life unfolds moment by moment! If my choice is for a full spiritual life, and I have consciously promised God to pursue this goal, I must give it my best and fullest attention. I do not, however, forget to look to the Lord for His strength. Recall repeatedly the wondrous deeds the Lord has done and live in creative fidelity and gratitude. Gratitude is a stance of a person who lives from the "inside out". It is the nature of a person who lives courageously—with the heart—and the whole of life exemplifies this.

Paul's reference to 'our hidden self' is a clue for us to be wary of confusing our spiritual formation with an abundance of practices, rote prayers, automatic almsgiving, lectures or workshops. These measureable things are sometimes used as the yardstick of our spirituality. Of course, these things may help because anyone or anything which supports the 'hidden self' to grow strong relates to our spiritual unfolding. But our growth in God must come from distilling and enhancing the God-life that is already mine.

The Main Portal—Prayer

There are many disciplines that can help us to live out our covenantal promise. A conscientious practice of prayer, or centering, is an absolute necessity. Personal prayer is the pursuit of the inward journey. It is the place where the voice of the heart becomes audible. We place ourselves in God's presence and quiet the self of all possible distractions. The beginning of each prayer time behooves us to ask the Holy Spirit for the grace to pray—for it is the Spirit within us that calls "Abba, Father". If we are true and faithful to prayer, we cannot help but experience that the fruits of the Holy Spirit will come alive in our lives. People may begin to wonder about our new found peace, joy, patience or gentleness and sensitivity to others. We will experience a sort of rejuvenation—new energy, kindness and love. Even currently, there are blogs on the internet reminding us of the value of prayer for healing and wholeness in our lives.

Though prayer is absolutely necessary for our spiritual growth, authentic prayer carries with it a great element of risk. It makes us vulnerable! We give ourselves into the hands of the Father who will challenge us to change our lives and perhaps even lead us in a direction we had not anticipated or intended.

The core self that I am, is overlaid with many layers of organic, emotional and ego dimensions which may prevent the authentic self from emerging. Periods of re-creative silence and stillness help to relativize these influences. They tend to remove, or lessen, some of the daily stress and strain. Then I am more apt to be drawn to the Holy as the Center of my life.

Have you ever reflected upon the question "Why did God create the Sabbath?" God knew from all eternity the bent of humans to be busy about so many things. When Jesus told Martha in the Sciptures[3] that Mary had chosen the better part, He was not disparaging hospitality and the work that it entails. He was merely reminding us to keep things in perspective. That is what 'Sabbath time' is meant to be, a time to get my perspectives once again in focus. We are called to let go of the hustle-bustle of our lives, to indulge in moments of prayer, silence, and reflectiveness. The Sabbath is a time to surrender to the calm, quiet awareness of the gift God wants to give. He repeats again and again in the depth of our hearts, "Come, aside and rest a while." How can we spurn such a genuine invitation? The Sabbath is a time to let the chaos of the week dissipate and disappear in the embrace of the Lord. Imagine how such a Sabbath could prepare one for a graced, gifted week, the memory of which could be balm for the spirit.

Primarily, our spiritual formation hinges on the truth that we are rooted in Christ. We have been baptized into Christ and that reality . . . that radical rootedness ushers us into the transformation which we pursue throughout our lives. Prayer renews that awareness. I realize very personally that a branch cannot bear fruit all by itself, but must remain part of the vine. (Cf. Jn. 15:4)

It is through prayer that I come to self knowledge which is the doorway to a deeper knowledge of God. It leads to an understanding and an ever-deepening awareness of my basic poverty. We learn, too, that self-knowledge is not an introspective, ego-centered dynamism. It is a movement beyond self in a gesture of love and concern. It is commonly called caring!

Meditation is the form of personal prayer that is a *sine qua non* for advancement along the spiritual path. It may take many forms. It may be reflection upon the Word of God. It may be a silent presence in the "centering" tradition which fastens my attention on God's presence within and about me. Teresa manifests a great freedom with prayer and methods of prayer. Her advice was to use whatever method worked for the individual. Teresa was more concerned about the effects of prayer than the method. It is this personal prayer that readies the heart for God's full sway in our lives. It is the uniting of the creature with the Creator—our earthiness with the Holy Creative Ground of our Being.

Journaling

Another of the most valued and powerful tools of spiritual growth, renewal and guidance, in our quest for personal knowledge and understanding, is reflection. At times it is necessary to dispose of old maps and methods to search for new routes or catalysts that will gently guide, or lovingly prod us to deeper awareness and insights.

Journaling is a mode of reflectiveness. It can reflect the current state of my spirit and also be a mode of centering and discipline. Especially after a busy day, a few moments of quiet in-gathering may be helpful. Journal keeping may be described as exteriorizing my inner emotions and thoughts, but it has also the gift of helping me to internalize—to listen to the call to "be more". Preferably, at a consistent time each day, I sit quietly and review the happenings of the day. One shuts down the activity of the day and opens one's self to God. This is accomplished through revisiting instances

M. GERMAINE HUSTEDDE, PHJC

scattered throughout the length and breadth of my day in the Light of the Holy. I simply write about an incident without trying to analyze or moralize about it. Perhaps it becomes a moment of truth in which I am dialoging with myself and the incident appears in a whole new light. In the book, The Help, Aibileen, one of the black maids, writes her prayers to God at the end of each day. This may be another form of journaling.

I like to compare journaling with basking in the sunshine. I sit in the light of God's grace and ponder an incident perhaps as ordinary as being embraced by a friend or loved one. It is against the backdrop of infinite love of God that I dare to look intensely at the wonder of my being and not get caught up or disturbed by the shadows which my same self casts.

Journaling can have both a deepening and cleansing effect. Facing myself quietly each day in a stance of gentle reflectivity may help me to face some issues I have skirted because of lack of time or reluctance to deal with them. I may dialogue with an event or reflect upon a relationship—with God or another. Maybe it will take the form of sketching a precious moment. I may give voice to a concern or be awed by my latest discovery. I may even explore a response or a non-response that was significant in my day.

After some months of journaling, I may go back and re-read my entries. They can teach me a lot about myself, for I will find that what I have written is not so new or startlingly different. Rather, I begin to see patterns of myself emerge: patterns of prayer, patterns of behavior, patterns of moods or of light-heartedness. These can be 'leading bands of love' drawing me to a deeper sense of who I really am at my deepest core.

Scriptural and Spiritual Reading

Another specific and helpful discipline is that of setting aside a time each day for Scriptural or spiritual reading. Return to the WORD with a listening ear. Certainly, we may not have hours for this practice, but ten or fifteen minutes can powerfully sustain me. Because a great deal of time is not available to me, I ought to be selective in my choices. I must also be a receptive, docile presence to the text before me. Susan Muto comments on my task as reader saying that we need to be present to the text in such a disciplined way that "emotions, prejudices and romantic feelings do not take over". I like her idea of allowing my deepest self to be awakened, such that it is my task to place myself at the disposal of the 'master'. In this way I allow myself to be led and transformed.[4]

Each page of Scripture offers the consoling and encouraging truth that God is concerned with individuals—not with faceless, nameless masses. God is concerned with ME!

In Scripture, the "master" who speaks to me is Christ Himself. The whole of Jesus' encounter with the Samaritan Woman at the Well (Jn. 4) is really about water and sustenance—but not merely physical water. Jesus is asking for a drink. True! However, the Biblical image is so much more that a cool drink on a hot day. Water was a sign of life, of salvation—"living water" which puzzled the Samaritan woman, so much. Jesus Himself wants to give us this 'life-giving water'. So often though, we focus on the 'lack of the bucket' that our vision cannot behold the gift God wants to give. In a Scripture passage such as this, I may find myself conversing with Jesus. Take the part of the puzzled woman and let the drama unfold for yourself. Wouldn't it be wonderful to have the scales fall from our eyes, as well as the haze that settles over us when we focus too much on the obvious?

I have found that pursuing Scriptural reading with a theme in mind (any concordance can help) brings a richness and challenge to me at the same time. The themes of journeying, of forgiveness, of waiting or watchfulness may open vistas for me that I have not yet explored. Each of these focuses me on the living God or the gentle Christ and helps me to understand more deeply the process I am in. It is through my focus again and again on the theme of waiting that I have fashioned my own motto for my spiritual process of commitment. I must remind myself repeatedly that I must be a patient and wait on the Lord. I must faithfully return to my motto and tell myself that it is mine to practice "Fidelity to the incomplete" in my life. The words God spoke to the Prophet Jeremiah, I have claimed as my own and through many years they have given me consolation, courage and conviction:

M. GERMAINE HUSTEDDE, PHJC

I have a plan for you says the Lord, plans for your welfare and not for your harm, to give you a future with hope. Then when you call upon me and come to pray to me, I will hear you.

When you search for me you will find me; if you seek me with all your heart.[5]

These words also reiterate a very special primordial conclusion. It is of greatest necessity that we seek God with 'all our heart'.

Sharing ones faith may also be a means of drilling further into one's depths. This consists primarily of telling someone, a companion or a trusted friend, how God has touched your life and the spring-board is usually a small, but significant Scripture passage. In allowing another to share her journey with me, I often find similarities that are encouraging, challenging and nourishment for my personal journey. Hopefully, my sharing does the same for a friend.

Spiritual Direction

For some, the guidance of a spiritual director or a spiritual companion may be a special aid in the living out of one's commitment. The director or companion may act as a mirror for me, reflecting back my feeble attempts, encouraging me and offering needed advice. In a Spiritual direction setting, I turn the earth, possibly plant some seeds, nurture and prune. I enter into my own truth with the Director such that I hear with sharpened perception and see with revealing light.

Though we have offered skeletal examples of means to help us grow in a personal relationship with our God, the most important thing to remember is that the development of this relationship is a process which requires absolute commitment, discipline and patience.

The life call of my God is an on-going summons and my response is the daily renewal of my commitment. I learn to live with my eyes open, ears attentive and with a malleable heart. The image of the Divine Potter is again very appropriate and it brings us full circle, ready to receive and welcome the Beloved . . . to allow His Presence to fill us to the brim and to rest in that Presence. There is no better way to grow in awareness of God's love than through Presence. It cannot be the 'roll call' presence which we experienced as students when merely occupying a given place fulfilled the role. Presence, in the spiritual sense is a determined awareness, a "being with" the Beloved in the present moment and of honoring that presence through respect, appreciation and reverence of all with whom I come in contact.

Just yesterday we had a priest, who was visiting us from Germany, celebrate Eucharist in our convent chapel. He commented that living a spiritual life is a matter of the heart. He went on to say, that the dialogue between the celebrant and the worshippers which precedes the Preface, contains an invitation to "Lift up your hearts", and we respond, "We have lifted them up to the Lord." In this simple one liner is the whole of the matter. We are invited to lift our hearts to our God and we respond with alacrity and love. This ought to be the rhythm and song of our day. It undergirds the prayer of 'Presence".

Throughout the day and throughout one's life we are invited to lift our hearts up to the Lord. Our actions, our readiness, openness, and attentiveness . . . all earmark the quality of our in-depth living. One evening in Africa, I was returning to my place of ministry after an all day meeting. Because we did not own a vehicle, I took advantage of the public mutatu (taxi) service. Usually there is space for ten or twelve passengers, but more often there are eighteen or twenty, especially if it is the last run of the day. Crowded together, and sitting partially on one's imagination, I happened to see the huge, vermillion full-moon just coming up over the horizon. It was picturesque and awesome over the barren landscape and the shrubs that etched a postcard look about it. After several minutes my delight spilled over, and I said aloud, "Oh, isn't that a beautiful sight!" The Councilman, from our District, was sitting next to me. Very matter of fact, he drily responded, "Yes, but who has eyes to see?"

The whole of life has built-in opportunities for returning to the center, for becoming aware of God's goodness and presence but they are easily overlooked. We fail to live in anticipation and the goal or need of the moment is so dangerously alluring. Unless, I develop a penchant for presence and inner stillness, I am liable to go through life with blinders which prevent me from seeing and relishing the goodness of God. The danger is that in my vacuum-like existence, I also forget my commitment to my God.

Because we are human, body, soul and spirit, worldly concerns will hang around to haunt us. But it is God's desire to grace us again as if it were the first Pentecost. The Holy Spirit has been given to us in Baptism and in the Sacrament of Confirmation. Let us allow the Spirit to enflame our entire being, for the essence of commitment is to have gratitude for the Redemptive Passion of Christ engraved in our hearts, the fire of the Spirit burning in our souls and the constant need to witness the awareness of God's love through my everyday walk with Him. It is my hope for you and my personal goal that together we come to the awesome gift of experiencing the spirituality of awakening and making room for our loving God.

NOTES:

1. Cf. Rev. 3: 15-17.
2. Cf. Paul Hinnebusch, <u>Religious Life: A Living Liturgy,</u> (New York: Sheed and Ward, 1965), p.159.
3. Cf. Lk. 10: 38-42.
4. Cf. Susan Annette Muto. <u>Approaching the Sacred: An Introduction to Spiritual Reading</u> (Denville, New Jersey: Dimension Books, 1973), p.17.
5. Jeremiah, 29: 11-14.

THE MOTHER AND THE CHILD

MOTHER GOD

I spend my day in the lap of God,
And when at mid-day the sun arched high
Has sprinkled gold dust wantonly
and gilded all the world—
I nestle closer to my God,
Content to be secure, yet free
In poverty and expectancy.

I know my pauper state—
Fully dependant, wanting all.
But with fixed faith and child's delight
The awareness of God's love
Imparts amazing insight!
The God who holds me, molds me.
In God, I come to be, authentic me.

FOR REFLECTION:

What is the poverty, the expectancy, that I experience in relationship to my God?

When have I felt God holding me?

In my process of 'authentic becoming' can I trust that God is the chief Player?

AFTER WORD

THE GERMAN LANGUAGE has a small phrase "Sitz in Leben". We could translate this as our 'point of departure.' My point of departure in writing this book has been that we are living in a favorable time, a kairos time, a time of opportunity in which we need but be hospitable to, and aware of the gift that we have, the Gift of Life. It is as though God stands at the door of each of us and says, "Open! I want to come in and celebrate this Gift with you." Only our deafness, indifference and busy-ness, or hardness of heart can refuse entrance to this Divine Guest.

It is my premise that anything and everything that happens in my life can be spiritually significant. Our entire life is an alchemy of the old and new, the eventful and uneventful, the dull and exciting, the happy and disappointing experiences . . . but nothing of it should be lost in the journey of our transformation.

I have tried to point out that we can live our lives so that spirituality can become part and parcel of our daily lived experience; that we can come to a mode of conversion in which we welcome and celebrate our very best selves. Living in an aura of wakefulness can pay dividends on our journey.

During the writing of this book, I mused, if Yahweh were to come to me today and ask me to sacrifice my dearest possession as he did ask Abraham, what is there in my life that I would be willing to part with? God told Abraham that it would be 'on the mountain' that He would point out to him what he was to sacrifice. Really, the time, the place and the gift itself, ALL is the prerogative of God Himself to decide. I came to the conclusion that it is not mine to say, but that in living I must be prepared to *give* whatever it is that God asks . . . to make room for God.

However, all of life is so dear that when we to come to the end of our days on this earthly journey our dear Lord will say to us, "Well, done! You have nourished and treasured the gift I have given you." This is concomitant with the daily ascent I make to the 'mount of decision'.

We want to live in the logic of existential knowing that all life is God's gift. My life is dear and precious . . . but there is more to it than meets the eye. It is my hope that the inner dimension of ourselves will be so treasured that the transformation which results fits us immanently for eternity but enables us also to live each day as a flowering forth into the wholeness and holiness that God desires and which delights us in the living of it.

We are the beloved daughters and sons of God our Father. That in itself is what makes us precious in God's eyes. In growing in this foundational premise we relish the relationship we forge with the Holy Other . . . and treasure the reality that all of life can be an encounter with our God. I have but to be hospitable to the Divine Who dwells with me.

BIBLIOGRAPHY

Berdyaev, Nicholas. *Spirit and Reality.* London: Geoffrey Bles. The Canterbury Press, 1939.

Blackman, H.J. *Six Existentialist Thinkers.* New York: Harper and Row Publishers, 1959.

Bloom, Anthony. *Living Prayer.* Springfield, Illinois: Templegate Publishers, 1966.

Bond, Raymond T. (ed.). The *Man Who Was Chesterton.* Garden City, New York: Doubleday and Company, 1960.

Collins, James. *The* Existentialists—*A Critique Study.* Chicago: Henry Regnery Company, 1952.

Crosby, Michael H. *Spirituality* of *the Beatitudes.* Maryknoll, New York: Orbis Books, 1981.

de Exupèry, Antoine. *The Little Prince.* New York: Harcourt, Brace and World, Inc., 1943.

del Mastro, M.L. *The Revelations of Divine Love in Sixteen Showings—Made to Julian of Norwich.* Liguori, MO: Triumph Books, 1994.

Dewey, Bradley R. *The New Obedience: Kirkegaard on Imitating Christ.* Washington, D.C.: Corpus Books, 1968.

Durwell, F.X. *The Redeeming Christ. Toward A Theology of Spirituality.* trans. Rosemary Sheed. New York: Sheed and Ward, 1963.

Eliot, T.S. *The Complete Poems and Plays 1909-1950.* New York: Harcourt, Brace and World, Inc., 1958.

———— *Murder In the Cathedral.* New York: Harcourt, Brace and World, Inc. 1935.

———— *Selected Poems.* New York: Harcourt, Brace and World, Inc., 1930.

Farrow, John. *The Story of Thomas More.* New York: Sheed and Ward, 1954.

Frankl Viktor. *Man's Search For Meaning, Revised and Updated.* New York: Washington Square Press, 1984.

Fromm, Erich. *The Art of Living.* New York: Harper and Row Publishers, 1956.

———— *Man For Himself.* New York: Holt, Rinehart and Winston, Inc. 1947.

Heidegger, Martin. *Being and Time.* trans. John Macquarrie and Edward Robinson. London: SCM Press, Ltd. 1962.

———— *Existence and Being.* Chicago: Henry Regnery Co., 1965.

Heschel, Abraham. "*The Older Person and the Family in the Perspective of the Jewish Traditon.*" Paper presented at the Whitehouse Conference on Aging Washington, D.C.: 1961.

Hesse, Herman. *Siddhartha*. trans. Hilda Rosner. New York: Bantam Books, 1991.

Hocking, Brian. *Biography or Oblivion*. Cambridge, MA: Schenkman Publ. Co., Inc. 1965.

Kraft, William. *The Search for the Holy*. Philadelphia: The Westminster Press. 1971.

Marcel, Gabriel. *Being and Having*. trans. Katherine Farrar. New York: Harper and Row Publishers. 1949.

———— *Metaphysical Journal*. trans. Bernard Wall. Chicago: Henry Regnery Company, 1952.

———— *The Mystery of Being II, Faith and Fidelity*. trans. Rene Hague. Chicago: Henry Regnery Company, 1951.

———— *The Philosophy of Existentialism*. trans. Manya Harari. New York: The Citadel Press, 1964

Maslow, Abraham H. *Toward a Psychology of Being*. Princeton, N.J.: van Nostrand Company, Inc. 1962.

Mauriac, Francois. *The inner Presence. Recollections of My Spiritual Life*. trans. Herma Briffault. New York: The Bobbs-Merrill Co., 1965.

———— *The Viper's Tangle*. trans. Warren B. Wells. New York: Sheed and Ward, 1947.

Metz, Johannes. *Poverty of Spirit*. trans. John Drury. Paramus, N.J.: Newman Press, 1968.

Moroux, Jean. *I Believe: The Personal Structure of Faith.* trans. Michael Turner. New York: Sheed and Ward, 1959.

_____ *The Meaning of Man.* trans. A.H.G. Downes. New York: Sheed and Ward, 1952.

Muto, Susan Annette, *Approaching the Sacred: An Introduction to Spiritual Reading.* Denville, New Jersey: Dimension Books, 1973.

_____ *Blessings That Makes US Be. A Formative Approach to Living the Beatitudes.* Pittsburg, PA: Epiphany Books, 2001.

Otto, Rudolph. *The Idea of the Holy.* trans. John W. Harvey. London: Oxford University Press, 1923.

Patka, Frederich, *Values and Existence: Studies in Philosophical Anthropology.* New York: Philosophical Library, 1964.

Paton, Alan. *Cry, the Beloved Country.* New York: Charles Scribner's Sons,1948.

Sheean, Vincent. *Lead Kindly Light.* New York: Random House, 1949.

Tagore, Rabindranath. *Collected Poems and Plays of Rabindranath Tagore.* London: Macmillan London Limited, 1947.

_____ *The Religion of Man.* Boston: Beacon Press, 1961.

Thoreau, Henry David. *Walden.* Boston Houghton, Mifflin CO., 1957.

Thorne, Dorothy Gilbert. *Poetry Among Friends.* Lebanon, PA: Sowers Printing Company, 1963.

Tillich, Paul. *The Courage To Be*. New Haven, Conn.: Yale University Press, 1952.

van Croonenburg, Engelbert. *Gateway to Realty: An Introduction to Philosophy*. Pittsburg: Duquesne University Press, 1968.

van Ewijh, Thomas J. *Gabriel Marcel: An Introduction*. Glen Rock, New Jersey, "Paulist Press, 1965."

van Kaam, Adrian, *Personality Fulfillment in the Spiritual Life*. Wilkesbarre, PA: Dimension Books, 1966.

van Zeller, Herbert. *The Current of Spirituality*. Sprngfield, IL: Templegate Publishers, 1970.

Wordsworth, William. *"Lines From Tintern Abbey" Major British Writers Enlarged Edition II*. New York: Harcourt, Brace and World, Inc., 1954.

Wigoder, Goffrey, (Gen. ed.) *Illustrated Dictionary and Concordance of the Bible*. G.G,: The Jerusalem Publishing House, Ltd. 1986.

Wright, Wm. Aldis. (ed.) *The Complete Works of Wm. Shakespeare*. New York: Doubleday and Company, Inc., 1936.

Edwards Brothers Malloy
Thorofare, NJ USA
August 29, 2014